# BIZARRE CANADA

## Wonderfully Weird & Hilarious

D0995609

Joanna Emery

BLUE
BIKE
BOOKS

The Publisher: Blue Bike Books

Website: www.bluebikebooks.com

Library and Archives Canada Cataloguing in Publication

Emery, Joanna
     Bizarre Canada: wonderfully weird & hilarious / Joanna Emery.

Includes bibliographical references.
ISBN 978-1-926700-24-3

     1. Canada—Miscellanea. I. Title.
FC60.E54 2010                971                C2010-901851-6

*Project Director:* Nicholle Carrière
*Project Editor:* Jordan Allan
*Cover Images:* photos.com
*Illustrations:* Roger Garcia, Peter Tyler, Patrick Hénaff, Graham Johnson, Djordje
          Todorovic
*Photography Credits:* Every effort has been made to accurately credit the sources of
photographs. Any errors or omissions should be reported directly to the publisher for
correction in future editions. Photographs courtesy of Dreamstime.com (p.32, p.70,
p.88, p.161, p.202, p.211); Joanna Emery (p.12, p.17, p.49, p.57, p.67, p.93, p.118,
p.128, p.131, p.137, p.138, p.139, p.145, p.149, p.154, p.162, p.168, p.187, p.198, p.199,
p.204, p.235, p.250, p.252, p.259, p.265, p.276); Cameron Stewart, Sign Maker,
District of North Vancouver (p.16); Vaughn Hamm, (p.42); Used by permission of
the Canadian Taxpayers Federation, www.taxpayer.com (p.44); Bud Bray (p.59);
William Jamieson, www.head-hunter.com (p.63); Jim Cornall, Huntsman Marine
Science Centre, www.huntsmanmarine.ca, (p.163); Courtesy of the Town of Vulcan,
www.vulcantourism.ca (p.270).

We acknowledge the support of the Alberta Foundation for the Arts for our publishing
program.

We acknowledge the financial support of the Government of Canada through the Book
Publishing Industry Development Program (BPIDP) for our publishing activities.

   Canadian    Patrimoine
Heritage    canadien

# DEDICATION

*To my family, Greg, Veronica, Monty and especially my little Mimi—I know I've dedicated all my books to you, and if I knew how many I'd actually write in my lifetime, I'd have done the "one at a time" thing.*

*To my friends—thank you for being there for me, as unconventional as I am.*

*To my pets—a heartfelt thanks to the ones who meowed and sat on my lap, and a special, chin scratch and belly rub to Zeus, our gentle giant St. Bernard, whom we love so dearly, despite his massive drools.*

*And finally for everyone who, like me, enjoys being a bit different…*

# CONTENTS

# ACKNOWLEDGEMENTS

A gazillion (yes, that bizarre word *is* real because my spell check didn't flag it) thanks to those who helped me put this book together, including my publisher and my dedicated editor, Jordan Allan, as well as everyone at Blue Bike Books—you are all the best!

Thanks to my family and friends for their support, patience and the countless meals they served me at the computer. Many thanks to those who answered my out-of-the-blue requests for information and photographs—I'm so glad there are generous people like you out there. You are (in no particular order): Cameron Stewart and the good folk at the District of North Vancouver, Vulcan Alberta Tourism, Jim Cornall and Jessica Richards at the Huntsman Marine Science Centre, Shirley Lowe and the Old Strathcona Business Association, Dean Smith and the Canadian Taxpayers Federation, Corran Addison, William Jamieson, Ruth McConnell, Mark D'Amore, Gary Duschl, Bud Bray, Vaughn Hamm, Michael Baldasaro and the Church of the Universe, and the many others behind the scenes….muchas gracias!

# INTRODUCTION

When I got the opportunity to have a book published about the bizarre aspects of Canada, I was thrilled. Strange is my middle name (okay, it's not really, but you know what I mean). I've always been one to collect offbeat, oddball and off-the-wall news to tell my family, and I admit, I'm always *glued* to the latest headlines—though too much of today's news is enough to put anyone in the looney bin. If we're not about to be hit by a bus crossing the road, keel over from salmonella poisoning or go bankrupt because we can't pay our bills, well, there's always December 12, 2012, to put an end to everything (I'm still researching that one).

Yet *strange* news, the unusual stuff that makes its way as little tidbits onto our television, radio and Internet, now *that* keeps me going. When you hear something completely out of the ordinary—like the guy who was charged with public drunkenness for performing CPR on a road-kill opossum, which actually happened, albeit in the United States and not in Canada—now *that* puts a smile on my face (apologies to the opossum).

In this book, I've tried to take the "best of the bizarre" in Canada. How does one define something that is "bizarre"? Even the dictionaries differ. Flip through various lexicon reference tools and you'll find "odd or unusual, especially in an interesting or amusing way" to "unconventional" or "outlandish," "out of the ordinary" or "unworldly." Get the picture? In a nutshell, "bizarre" means weird, and that can often be very subjective. Bizarre might describe a place, object, event or even a person (who may be on or off certain medications or non-prescription drugs). It might even describe you, especially in the wee hours of a weekend morning.

As for Canada, this wonderful country is not immune to the bizarre bug. As you read through these pages, I think you'll agree. We've got enough craziness to cover every square metre of our great land, and that's *a lot* of surface area! One thing everyone will agree on is that bizarre things make this world more interesting, even downright fun—and we could all use a little more fun in our lives. Long live the bizarre in us all!

# NUTTY NAMES

*I am rather inclined to believe that this is the land
God gave to Cain.*

–Jacques Cartier, when he reached the north shore of
the Gulf of St. Lawrence, 1534

*Perhaps Jacques Cartier had a point; he was, after all,
staring at a rather imposing outcrop of rock. But for
those of us who have actually seen more of this land,
and for those of us who don't get all our history from
Tragically Hip lyrics, we know Canada is one awesome
country—it's just a little, well, different. Where else
can you ask for directions to Blow Me Down or Crotch
Lake and not get slapped? Yes, we're freaky from far and
wide…and proud of it!*

## Nope, Nothing Here

Most of us learned in elementary school that the name "Canada"
is derived from the Aboriginal word for village, *Kanata*. It may
also be from the Spanish phrase *aca nada*, which means "oh, there's
nothing here." The First Nations, who may have had contact with
Aboriginal peoples from farther south, repeated the words to the
French when they arrived. The French mistook the phrase and
thought they had reached a land called "Canada."

### Welcome to Efisga

Be grateful we live in a country with the name "Canada." It could
have been, believe it or not, "Efisga." Trust me, I am not making
this up. Dozens of other suggestions were bantered around, including New Britain, Britannia, Columbia, Laurentia, Ursalia, Vesporia,
and the always infectious, Canadia. A few of our founding fore-
fathers thought the country should be called Cabotia, in honour

of explorer John Cabot, or after royalty, such as Victorialand or Albertoria. The latter two were nixed as they wouldn't have made the French very happy. Other perplexing propositions included Niagarentia (which could have been a boon for tourism), Transatlantica, Norland (can you imagine everyone confusing us with Norway?) and Tupona, which stood for The United Provinces of North America. Then there's Efisga, an acronym of the six main homelands: England, France, Ireland, Scotland, Germany and Aboriginal. I can hear it now, "O Efisga, our home and native land…"

## The Kingdom of Canada

Legally today, we're called "Canada," but when the British North America Act took effect on July 1, 1867, we officially became the "Dominion of Canada." For a fleeting moment, it was thought the "Kingdom of Canada" might be a better term, but someone wisely pointed out the Americans would likely feel uneasy living next to a "kingdom." Eventually, "Dominion" was phased out, and Dominion Day was changed to Canada Day in 1982.

**Question:** *Where was the British North America Act signed?*
**Answer:** *At the bottom.*

## Make a Left at Eyebrow...

There's a story behind each one of the thousands of oddly named places in Canada. Take for instance, Regina, Saskatchewan, which was once named Pile O' Bones after the buffalo bones left behind by the Cree. Lethbridge, Alberta, was originally called Fort Whoop-Up by settlers and later Coal Banks, while Hairy Hill was named after the clumps of buffalo hair that were left on bushes by the once-common bovines. Then there's the northern Ontario town of Swastika, incorporated in 1908; its residents were proud of their town's moniker. The swastika was actually an ancient good luck symbol before the Nazis perverted it. After World War II, politicians were a little hypersensitive over other names too, like Berlin, Ontario. That city took the name Kitchener, and Swastika was slated to become the town of Winston, after Winston Churchill. The townsfolk successfully fought the change, and lucky Swastika prevailed.

## Yer Favourites

Travel off the beaten track and you're bound to run into an off-beat place name. Here's a sample of real Canadian places with really weird names:

### Newfoundland

- Blow Me Down
- Dildo
- Mosquito
- South Dildo
- Too Good Arm
- Come-By-Chance
- Jerry's Nose
- Nameless Cove
- Snooks Arm
- Witless Bay

**Nova Scotia**
- Ecum Secum
- Malignant Cove
- Garden of Eden
- Mushaboom

**Québec**
- Asbestos
- Saint-Louis-du-Ha! Ha!
- Mayo

Saint-Louis-du-Ha! Ha!

**Ontario**
- Crotch Lake
- Ochiichagwe'babigo'ining
- Tiny
- Frogmore
- Swastika

**Manitoba**
- Gods Lake

**Saskatchewan**
- Eyebrow
- Uranium City
- Fertile

**Alberta**
- Czar
- Hairy Hill
- Dead Man's Flats
- Legal

**British Columbia**
- Blubber Bay
- Stoner
- Skookumchuck
- Spuzzum

# THE TRUE NORTH STRONG AND STRANGE

## Planetary Stand-ins

Devon Island in Nunavut is dry, cold and rock-filled. But one man's desolate wilderness is another man's ideal research area. NASA used this region north of Baffin Island as the perfect place to test its Mars experiments in the 1990s. Canada has always been a favourite testing ground of NASA's. The Space Agency used to practice moonwalks in the barren landscape surrounding Sudbury. But that's ancient history, right? Nickel refining may have caused the area to turn into a moonscape back then, but now, thanks to reforestation and environmental action, Sudbury is a much greener city, thank you.

## Being on Alert

If you have to work in Alert, you might as well live there. If you lived in the nearest city, Iqaluit, the commute to Alert would be a killer. Situated at the tip of Ellesmere Island, Alert is the most northerly permanently inhabited place in the world. Iqaluit, Nunavut's capital, is about 2092 kilometres south. To put that in perspective, the North Pole is an easier jaunt at only 800 kilometres away. Originally a weather station in 1950, Alert is now a Canadian Forces station where about five dozen military and Environment Canada staff live and work. From mid-October until the end of February, it's dark virtually all of the time, but that changes from the end of March to mid-September, when it's constantly daytime.

Visit the Western Arctic Regional Visitor Centre in Inuvik and you'll get a special freebie. The "Certificate of the Arctic Circle Chapter, Order of Adventurers" proves you've crossed the Arctic Circle. And it's guaranteed to make your friends wish they had one, too.

# SIGNS, SIGNS, EVERYWHERE A SIGN

## Look for the Broken Tree Branch

Where would we be without signs to tell us where to go? Very lost indeed. One of the first signposts was the tree trail marker. The limb of a young tree along a path was tied down or partially broken in order to point in the direction one should go. As the tree limb grew, it permanently pointed the way. In the Arctic, the Inuit built *inukshuks*—or stone piles shaped like a human being—to show where to fish or find shelter. Nowadays, Canadian street signs are in English or French, English *and* French, English and Inuktitut (if you're in Nunavut), or a myriad of other numbers, letters and images, depending on where you are.

## A Is for Alpha

Travel through the rural prairies and you might notice an unusual twist with the town name signs. For instance, there's Fenwood, Goodeve, Hubbard, Ituna…hmm, get the picture? What a sensible idea—name your towns alphabetically and no one gets lost! That's exactly what the Grand Trunk Railway Company did in the late 19th century as it established stations along its tracks. Today, many of the communities that grew up around those railway stations have kept the names, from Arona in Manitoba to Zeneta in Saskatchewan. As for the alphabetical gaps, those are the places where some towns have dwindled away over time.

ODDLY ENOUGH

A sign heading into Biggar, Saskatchewan, portrays the official town motto: "New York is Big, but This is Biggar."

## Slow Down, Elephants Crossing

No doubt we've all seen those deer, moose and turtle crossing signs, but the District of North Vancouver, BC, has gone one further. In an effort to get drivers to slow down and watch for wildlife, the city set up street signs that actually indicate a deer crossing but depict the silhouetted image of an elephant, camel or rhino instead. The double-take signs are the work of North Vancouver sign maker Cameron Stewart. Feedback about his tongue-in-cheek creations has been so positive that even London, England, has copied the idea for a few of their parks. Nothing like a little humour to put people, especially motorists, in a good mood.

## Anyone Have a GPS Here?

Drive south from Whitehorse for about a day to the town of Watson Lake, Yukon, and you will wonder which way to turn next when you arrive at one particular corner called the Signpost Forest. This signage congestion began in 1942 when Carl K. Lindley, an American army engineer working on the Alaska Highway, decided to put up a sign pointing to his home town of Danville, Illinois. The idea caught on, and now there are more than 14,000 signs pointing in virtually every direction.

Highway sign near the author's home in Southern Ontario.

# SURVIVOR, CANADA

*Canada is so far away, it hardly exists.*

–Jorge Borges, South American author and poet

## Vanished, Forever

The Beothuk peoples were experts when it came to surviving in Canada, at least until the Europeans arrived. For two millennia, the Beothuk lived in the area known today as Newfoundland and Labrador. Tall and dark-haired, they were eventually forced from their habitat by settlers in the 1700s and quickly succumbed to white-man diseases. In 1823, three Beothuk women were found and only one, named Shanawdithit, survived. When she died of tuberculosis at age 26 in 1829, the Beothuk had essentially been wiped off the face of the planet, never to return.

### Alex Wuz Here

Alexander Mackenzie, like many explorers, was in Canada looking for a way to get to China. At one point, he found a long river that he thought might take him where he wanted to go—but no such luck. Mackenzie's "River of Disappointment" was later renamed the Mackenzie River. He tried again and ended up on the shores of the Pacific Ocean near Bella Coola on July 22, 1793. How do we know? In a word: graffiti. Mackenzie wrote his name and the date in a reddish paint of vermillion and bear grease on a boulder. The Mackenzie Rock, now permanently etched with Mackenzie's original inscription "Alex Mackenzie from Canada by land 22 July 1793," can still be seen at Sir Alexander Mackenzie Provincial Park.

### Henry "Rock" Hudson

In 1960, workers repaving a highway at Deep River near Chalk River found a large granite boulder with the inscription "H.H. 1612 CAPTIVE" carved into it. Did the initials "H.H." stand for the British explorer, Henry Hudson? In 1611, Hudson was famously set adrift in James Bay with his son and seven faithful sailors after his crew mutinied. Could he have made his way down the Ottawa River and been captured by Native persons? While the scenario is unlikely, it's not entirely impossible. The stone was put on display in a park at Chalk River in 1998 but was smashed into four pieces by vandals a few weeks later. Fortunately, the inscription was not damaged, but whether Henry Hudson was the one who etched those letters still remains a mystery.

## Been Here, Found That

If you think the first European to explore the coast of what was to become British Columbia was Captain James Cook in the 1700s, think again. In 1579, English explorer Sir Francis Drake may have actually sailed at least as far as the Queen Charlotte Islands. El Draco—"The Dragon," as Drake was called by his arch rivals, the Spanish—may have secretly altered his official maps of the Pacific Coast so as not to tip off the competition. If true, which new evidence shows may very likely be the case, then it's time to update those history books.

### So How Was the Trip?

No wonder Canada is seen as a wild, untamed land. More than a few wandering explorers have ended up lost or, even worse, dead. Take the famous Franklin Expedition led by Sir John Franklin. Sir John was an efficient and hardy commander. He had already explored the Arctic and even ate his boots to survive one particularly gruelling voyage. When Sir John left England in 1845 to search for the elusive Northwest Passage through the Arctic Ocean, his two ships, the HMS *Terror* and HMS *Erebus*, were stocked with supplies, including clothing, desks and even an organ. More importantly, they had the latest invention in high-tech foodstuffs (well, high tech for the 19th century): tinned cans. At least 8000 cans of food were loaded onto the ships to keep the crew of 130 happy and well fed. Unfortunately, the Franklin Expedition never did return from its voyage, and the ships were last spotted around Baffin Bay.

Over the next several years, search crews tried to piece together what had happened. They found spoons, empty cans, and later, grisly skeletons of the remaining crewmembers. Cut marks on their bones revealed that they had resorted to cannibalism after all the food ran out. The crew, though, never had much of a chance because their food was slowly poisoning them. The process by which the cans were sealed involved using a solder that was 90 percent lead and may have seeped into the food. Symptoms of lead poisoning included confusion and weakness. Hair samples taken from the bodies of Franklin's men have since been proven to contain over 100 times the safe amount of lead. It's believed that Franklin's ships became locked in ice, and over time, crewmembers succumbed to the symptoms of lead poisoning.

And this wasn't the last time famished Arctic explorers resorted to, ahem, rare human steak. In 1881, the ill-fated Greely Expedition ended up with survivors also being forced to eat not only their shoes but their dead as well.

# SLEEPING NEXT TO THE ELEPHANT

*God Bless America, but God help Canada to put up with them.*

–Anonymous

## Oops, Sorry About the Battle

Good news didn't travel very fast in 1815. The War of 1812 between the United States and the British Empire (as in, Canada before Confederation) ended with the Treaty of Ghent on December 24, 1814. Unfortunately, military forces didn't get the memo, and the Battle of New Orleans happened in early January 1815, causing hundreds of unnecessary casualties. The British fought back at the Battle of Fort Bowyer on February 12, 1815. When they finally received word of the peace treaty, they promptly went home.

### Did the American Revolution Help Create Canada?

It's possible that without the United Empire Loyalists, what is now called Canada would not have been able to resist a vigorous expansion by the United States. While the Loyalists weren't only English—many were German, Scottish, Irish, French and Dutch—they helped ensure that Canada had safety in numbers. During the American Revolution, about 100,000 colonists who remained true to the British government left for Canada, Florida, Jamaica and the Bahamas. At the start of the War of 1812, there were tens of thousands of American-born settlers living in Upper Canada. Colonial cultural baggage aside, it's highly likely that without the Loyalists, we Canadians would all be singing "The Stars and Stripes Forever"!

# Straddling the Border

A black boundary line runs right through the Haskell Free Library and Opera House located right smack on the border of Stanstead, Québec, and Derby Line, Vermont. Technically, you can have one foot in the United States and one in Canada at the same time. Or sit in the American half of the opera seats and watch the stage over there in Canada. Built in 1904 by a married couple (yes, one was American and the other Canadian), it's the only public place in the world situated on a border. But don't think it's an easy

way to get into another country—Big Brother is still watching. Residents of the two towns have seen some changes since the terrorist attacks of September 11, 2001. Gate barriers, passport checks and increased security have meant the locals are more restricted in their border crossing than previous years.

Dr. Soloman Secord, a surgeon and the great-nephew of Laura Secord, left Kincardine, Ontario, to fight for the South in the American Civil War with the 20th Georgia Infantry. Despite being an abolitionist, he was captured at Gettysburg in 1863 but later escaped. Dr. Secord returned to Kincardine in 1864, where a monument in his honour still stands today, the only monument in honour of a Confederate officer in Canada. No mention, though, about whether or not he liked chocolate.

## Hey, Let's Invade the USA!

Believe it or not, Canada actually drafted plans to invade the United States. Okay, it was more along the lines of "how not to be invaded by the United States," but still. In the 1920s, Lieutenant Colonel James "Buster" Sutherland Brown wrote a paper entitled "Defence Scheme Number 1," whereby Canada would quickly occupy strongholds such as Seattle and Albany to buy time until the British Army could swoop in and save us all. Fiercely loyal to the British government, Brown had always been somewhat suspicious of the renegade United States. What if there was a war between Britain and the U.S.? Shouldn't Canada have a contingency plan?

Brown was later dismissed as director of Military Operations and Intelligence at Canadian Army Headquarters. By 1931, the scheme was dropped altogether. Everyone realized that if such a war actually *did* occur, the Americans would easily win. As it turned out, the Americans had drafted their own "U.S. Army Strategic War Plan Red" in the 1930s, which called for occupation of key Canadian cities such as Halifax, Québec City, Montréal, Toronto and Vancouver in the event of an attack on North American soil. In the 1980s, a British newspaper, *The Telegraph*, decided to use this scenario in a fake news story as part of an April Fools' Day joke. Pretty funny, except for the scary reality that it was all based on fact.

# GOOD IDEA, BAD IDEA

*You know, that these two nations [France and England]
have been at war over a few acres of snow near Canada,
and that they are spending on this fine struggle more than
Canada itself is worth.*

–Voltaire, *Candide*, chapter 23

*Most Canadians will agree—Canada is much more than
just "a few acres of snow." It's millions of acres of snow!
But seriously, running a country can't be easy, and there
have definitely been some bumps along the way. Then
again, they do say we get the government we deserve.
Ah, come on, we're not that bad, are we?*

## We Turned 'Em Down

Does Canada have a thing against warm tropical islands? After
World War II, Great Britain thought Canada might like to take
over responsibility of the West Indies. We said no, and eventually the islands, except for the British Virgin Islands, gained
their independence. At one point, even Dominica, the island
north of Barbados, wanted to join Canada. Again, we said sorry,
but no thanks. In 1987, the Canadian Parliament once again
turned down a request by the beautiful Caribbean Turks and
Caicos to join our northern Confederation, despite the fact that
90 percent of the 10,000 islanders supported the notion. The
effort was restarted in 2003, but so far the Canadian government has given the idea the cold shoulder. Perhaps we need to
chill out for a few more winters, eh?

# That's ONE CRAZY CANUCK! Louis Riel

Hero or traitor? Sinner or saviour? Louis Riel, the Métis leader of rebellions in 1869 and 1885, is certainly a controversial figure. To the First Nations, who put up with smallpox, railways through their land and fewer buffalo, Riel was an ally. To the government, who quashed the rebellion in 1869 and later the North West Rebellion, Riel was a pain in the neck.

Riel was eventually executed for his actions, but was it a mistake? For one, his lawyer wanted him to plead insanity. Secondly, even the jury didn't think Riel was bad enough for the gallows. "We, on the jury, recommend mercy," they announced. "The prisoner was guilty…but we felt that the government had not done its duty. It did nothing about the grievances of the Métis. If it had, there would never have been a second Riel rebellion." And lastly, some argue Riel was not a Canadian citizen at the time of the rebellions. He had become an American citizen, so how could he be guilty of treason against Canada? Makes no sense to me.

## Riel's Roots

Louis Riel was born in Red River, Manitoba, but traced his roots and strong will back to one tough grandmother from Québec City. Her name was Marie-Anne Gaboury, and she married a young, adventurous fur trader named Jean-Baptiste Lagimodière. They soon had a baby boy, but that didn't stop Marie-Anne from following her husband as a voyageur from Montréal to Lake Superior, across present-day North Dakota and later Alberta. Did I mention Marie-Anne was also pregnant with their second child during this time? At one point, an Assiniboine chief offered the couple several horses in exchange for their attractive little boy, but they refused. Later, while Jean was required to be away fur trading, Marie-Anne was left alone in a small cabin with her three children. After 14 months, Jean finally returned, and they eventually settled near the Red River. Jean lived to be 76, and Marie survived until age 95. The couple's daughter, Julie, was Riel's mother.

In 1868, one short year after the birth of Canada, Joseph Howe, a proud Nova Scotian, went to Britain to try to get Confederation repealed. He didn't succeed.

# It's Not Funny

Joey Smallwood, Newfoundland's first premier, bristled when he learned of the scheduled date of Newfoundland's official entry into Confederation: April 1, 1949. While this date, which, as everyone knows, is April Fools' Day, may have been picked as the start of the fiscal business year, Smallwood didn't want his province to be the butt of any jokes and wisely moved the date to March 31, 1949.

> **Question:** *What is the smartest province in Canada?*
> **Answer:** *Newfoundland and Labrador, because it has four "A"s and a "B."*

# CEREMONIALLY INCORRECT

## Making a Mace

The mace is an odd-looking object with a long history. Centuries ago, maces were spiky, lethal weapons used mainly in battle, but kings or bishops often possessed a special gold or jewel-encrusted mace just to show off. Gradually, the mace became a symbolic part of royal ceremonies. In the Canadian Parliament, the mace was originally incorporated for the protection of the Speaker of the House (it's unclear if any hecklers were ever bonked over the head) and was eventually kept on as a traditional symbol. As per the custom, the mace *must* be present because it represented authority, power and getting down to business. When Alberta's First Provincial Legislature was ready for its first sitting in 1906, they suddenly realized they had an urgent problem—no mace! How could the Assembly get down to business without the presence of a ceremonial mace?

With only a few weeks until the big day, Rufus E. Butterworth was asked to fashion a temporary mace. To his credit, Rufus did a pretty good job. He scavenged items lying around the house (Home Depot wasn't around back then), including a plumbing pipe, a toilet tank float, old shaving mug handles (to decorate the "orb") and parts from an old bedstead. He then gave his craftwork a coat of gold paint, and voilá, a traditional (looking) mace! The makeshift mace was used for the opening ceremonies on March 15, 1906. It was supposed to be quickly replaced but hung around for the next 50 years. They sure don't make plumbing parts like they used to.

**Thou Shalt Not Use the Name Parliament Hill in Vain**
Don't even try to sell Parliament Hill Cookies in Canada. You can market them as Parliament Cookies, but including the "Hill" part will land you in very hot water. It is against the law to use the name "Parliament Hill" for commercial purposes thanks to a Private Member's Bill that resulted in the "Act Respecting the Use of the Expression 'Parliament Hill.'" The Act came into effect in 1972 after an Ottawa hotel wanted to call itself the Parliament Hill Hotel. In the end, the name Parliament Hotel was okay but not the Parliament Hill Hotel—such a moniker would have risked a fine of $2000 or six months in jail. Which begs the question, if you served the jail time in Ottawa, would you be staying at the "Hotel Parliament Hill"?

# MPs, Take Your Chairs

Since 1988, members of the House of Commons can actually buy their solid-oak, leather and velvet chairs when they resign from politics. Well, it's supposedly not the *real* chair but rather a replica. Many get a plaque with the member's name screwed onto the back, just to give it that personalized touch. There is a cost associated with this purchase, but procedural clerks at the research branch of the House of Commons were unable to find the actual price. Let's hope it wasn't too much of a bargain basement price.

## Historical Stains

Deep in the Library and National Archives in Ottawa are two signed originals of the 1982 Charter of Rights and Freedoms. One is slightly water-damaged from the raindrops on the day Canada's famous Bill of Rights was signed by Prime Minister Pierre Trudeau and Queen Elizabeth II. The other is stained with red ink, the result of a vandal who inked it while it was on display in 1983.

# LAW AND DISORDER

## You Can't Handle the Margarine

Will that be butter or margarine? The debate has been around since the non-dairy spread was first invented. In fact, until 1948 (and except for a few years after World War I), margarine was verboten in Canada. Over the years, most provinces gradually accepted yellow-dyed margarine, except for Québec. A fierce dairy lobby was out to fry any margarine sales and demanded that it not be the same colour as butter. It succeeded when the Québec government outlawed non-white margarine masquerading as the real thing from grocery shelves. Tubs of the now-illegal spread that were smuggled into small grocery stores were seized under the law. After 21 years and a decade of court cases, Québec changed its mind in 2008 and finally allowed butter-coloured margarine. Consumers rejoiced and toasted their new freedom of choice.

## One Woman, One Vote

*...no woman, idiot, lunatic or criminal shall vote.*

–Dominion Elections Act, 1906

While it sounds ridiculous today, many people in the 19th and early 20th century thought that if women could vote, it would lead to marriage breakdowns and chaos on the home front. Understandably, more than a few Canadian women were peeved at the conditions of the Elections Act. In 1914, author Nellie McClung and members of the suffrage movement protested the fact that women weren't allowed to vote. They held a "mock parliament" in Manitoba, where McClung put the shoe on the other foot, so to speak, and pretended the roles were reversed. If it were *men* who were seeking the right to vote, all hell might break loose. She declared, "Politics unsettles men and unsettled men mean

unsettled bills, broken furniture, broken vows and divorce. Men's place is on the farm." McClung had the audience roaring with laughter. By 1920, women in Canada were given the same federal voting rights as men, but certain religious and racial groups, such as Asians and Aboriginals, remained excluded from the franchise.

## Truth and Justice

If you ever stroll outside the steps of the Supreme Court of Canada building in Ottawa, be sure to check out the two statues, Veritas and Justitia. Their names stand for Truth and Justice, and they were created by Toronto artist Walter S. Allward. Allward also designed the Canadian War Memorial at Vimy Ridge and the Alexander Graham Bell monument in Brantford, Ontario. He made Veritas and Justitia during the 1920s, but they were packed away for 50 years until 1969 when they were finally rediscovered in crates in an Ottawa parking lot!

## The Doobie Sacrament

To members of the Church of the Universe in Canada, the marijuana plant represents the "tree of life" and is no less than a holy sacrament. Think about getting high on incense, spreading that nice, easy feeling—you get the picture. The Church of the Universe was formed in 1969 near Hamilton, Ontario, by Reverend Brother Walter Tucker, who envisioned a more peaceful, groovy world. Reverend Brother Michael Baldasaro, a current Church leader, remains active in the community and has even run, unsuccessfully, for mayor of Hamilton several times. The Church only has two rules: do not hurt yourself and do not hurt others. Partaking in the sacrament (meaning smoking a joint) is encouraged, even though every once in a while a member is charged with trafficking. The Church, which has more than 4000 members across Canada, argues that charging their members is an infringement of their freedom of religion under the Charter of Rights. Members vow to take their fight to the Supreme Court one day, but for now, they're simply chilling out and taking deep breaths.

# Demonstrate Naked

There's one sure way to grab attention during a protest—take off all your clothes. It's all natural, and it's a part of Canadian history. In 1899, thousands of *Doukhobors*—Russian-speaking religious dissenters who resisted military conscription—travelled to Canada for a new life. They settled in Saskatchewan as well as in parts of Alberta and British Columbia. As pacifist Christians, they lived simply and asked only for the freedom to follow their beliefs. They did not, however, agree to swear allegiance to the Crown and submit to various Canadian laws. A small percentage of them, known as the "Sons of Freedom," staged their first nude protest in 1903. All the RCMP could do was arrest them for indecent exposure. In British Columbia, supporters of one of the imprisoned Sons of Freedom leaders rallied outside the jail proclaiming that "Jesus would not carry a gun."

## Bare-Breasted

On a sweltering summer day in 1991, university student Gwen Jacobs decided to remove her top while strolling through a public park in Guelph, Ontario. A few police officers asked her to cover up, but Jacobs replied that if men could walk around naked above the waist, why not women? She later sat topless outside on her porch. Another officer approached and asked her to put on her shirt, but Jacobs firmly refused. The officer noted that several beer-drinking fellows nearby were watching Jacobs with binoculars. Jacobs was arrested for indecent exposure, and the case went to court. After appeals, the court confirmed that Jacobs wasn't guilty of committing an indecent act. Her toplessness was non-commercial (translation: no money involved) and wasn't done for sexual purposes (translation: no hanky panky involved). The judge also noted that no one was forced to look at her.

## Getting a Bum Rap

Streakers, on the other hand, aren't usually so lucky, although one Ottawa streaker did receive an absolute discharge after dashing buck naked to the local beer store on a dare. Another streaker, who ran across a football field in Regina, had his conviction overturned on appeal—the judge noted that his indiscretion was met with "amused tolerance." Whew. On another occasion, seven young men in their birthday suits who ran toward the field during a 2007 Labour Day football game between the Calgary Stampeders and Edmonton Eskimos weren't so fortunate. Security somehow managed to grab hold of five of them, but two nudies slipped through and reached the turf. Police slapped them each with a charge of performing an indecent exhibition in a public place.

# IT DRIVES ME CRAZY

## Watch Out for the Demon Driver Priest

The first Canadian to drive was Father Georges-Antoine Belcourt of Prince Edward Island. In 1866, he bought a steam car from Philadelphia and drove this "horseless carriage" around during the St. Jean Baptiste Day ceremonies. According to *Cars of Canada*, Belcourt has the distinction of being "the first Canadian motorist, the first to buy a car and the first to import one." Parishioners, though, were not happy with this ungodly contraption, which scared their horses—they believed that the car was demon possessed.

 In 1903, car licence plates in Ontario were made of patent leather. When the Motor Vehicle Law went into effect in Nova Scotia in 1907, the one-time auto registration fee was a mere five dollars.

## Left, Right, Left

*…no automobile shall be driven through the streets of the Town of Digby at a speed exceeding six miles an hour and the drivers of the automobiles shall keep the horn sounding while approaching toward and passing any person driving, walking or standing upon the streets…*

–*Digby Weekly Courier*, July 1910

If Canada is a former British colony, why do we drive on the right? Since the first European settlements in Canada were originally French, most of Québec and parts of Ontario followed their lead and kept to the right. English areas of Atlantic Canada and later British Columbia, however, preferred the left.

With the advent of the automobile in the early 20th century, the situation became a lot more complicated. Officially, British Columbia and New Brunswick didn't switch to driving on the right until 1922. Nova Scotia waited until April 15, 1923, for its road-side conversion. Motorists put metal signs on their windshields to remind them to "Keep to the Right." Cart-pulling oxen, which had always been trained to walk on the left, took the change the hardest. Many of the older, more stubborn beasts were sent to slaughter after being replaced by younger, more trainable oxen. Oversupply meant meat prices dropped dramatically, and Lunenberg County declared 1923 to be the "Year of Free Beef."

## All the Rage

We've all seen the headlines: one driver tailgates or cuts another driver off. The cars stop, the drivers emerge and any sense of civility goes out the window. Nowhere are incidences of road rage more common than on the streets of Toronto. It's a war zone out there, especially when automobiles, pedestrians and bicyclists all share the road. By the third week of January 2010 alone, more than a dozen pedestrians had already been killed in Canada's biggest city. Ironically, the year before had seen the lowest number of traffic fatalities in almost 50 years. In Montréal, however, targeted pedestrian safety programs in spring and fall have helped substantially lower the jaywalking collision rate.

Cycling in cities, however, isn't any safer. When the price of fuel jumps, more people cycle to work to save money. At least 10 percent of all collisions between bicycles and vehicles are the ubiquitous "door prizes," that is, an automobile door opened in the path of a moving bicycle. Usually, it's the motorist who escapes unhurt. And then there's bike rage. In January 2006, a cyclist observed a driver stuck in traffic toss his half-eaten Jamaican patty out the car window. The cyclist opened the car door and threw it right back in. The driver retaliated by throwing two cups of hot coffee back at her. A fist fight then ensued until bystanders finally broke it up. It's enough to make you wonder why we can't all just get along.

## Car Kafuffle

*Drivers of horses are mostly on business, but the "devil wagons" are used for fun. Has the whole county, whose people built the roads for their own use in order to do their work, to put up with these pleasure jaunters?*

−New Glasgow Eastern Chronicle, June 1907

Although most of Canada, and especially the United States, was thrilled with the arrival of the automobile, PEI wasn't. In 1905, there were at least five cars on the island, but they disrupted regular island life, causing near accidents, spooking horses and spewing smoke. In a predominantly rural area, cars were seen as a luxury for the rich. Animosity grew against the "devil wagons," and in 1908, automobiles were prohibited on the island. Five years later, the New Automobile Act came into effect, and cars were permitted to travel the roads on Monday, Wednesday and Thursday. By 1918, cars were again allowed to operate seven days a week.

# MPs BEHAVING BADLY

### Rude-a-Thon

In the spring of 1878, during an all-night debate in the House of Commons, Members of Parliament truly left their manners at home. Interruptions included blowing trumpets, pounding on desks, as well as throwing paper missiles, books and toy balloons in the air. Others broke out into songs such as "Auld Lang Syne" and "God Save the Queen" during the 27-hour debate. Clearly, nothing much has changed.

## Stupid Airport Stunts

*I'm no lady. I'm an MP.*

–Agnes McPhail

Want to know what *not* to do at an airport? Just ask an MP. In 1991, Tory cabinet minister Alan Redway joked he had a gun while boarding a flight. After charges were laid, Redway resigned. Helena Guergis, Minister of State for the Status of Women, wasn't in a good mood the night of her birthday in February 2010. Guergis arrived minutes before her flight from Charlottetown was about to leave. When asked to remove her boots for security, she apparently threw them into the bin and swore at airport staff. Guergis later apologized through the media, but critics argued that if she wasn't an MP, she could have been arrested—or even tasered—for her temper tantrum.

### The Kitten Eater

During the 2003 Ontario election campaign, an email was sent out from the Conservatives calling Dalton McGuinty, the Liberal leader, an "evil reptilian kitten-eater from another planet." McGuinty denied ever eating kittens, but he did confess to having dined on calf.

# That's ONE CRAZY CANUCK! Jean Chrétien's Shawinigan Handshake

*For me, pepper, I put it on my plate.*

–Jean Chrétien, referring to an RCMP pepper-spraying incident

"Not you again!" said Queen Elizabeth when Prime Minister Jean Chrétien knocked on her door to speak about a constitutional matter. Thankfully, Queen Elizabeth was only joking. She was on good terms with Chrétien, who served as Canada's Prime Minister from 1993 to 2003. As for the rest of Canadians, well, he was one of those politicians you either loved or hated, but he certainly made headlines. Some of his actions make later leaders, such as Stephen Harper, more boring than a funeral procession. Take, for instance, Flag Day on Parliament Hill. Chrétien was making his way through a thick crowd when a protester started heckling him just inches from his face. Chrétien grabbed the fellow by the neck and pushed him to the ground. It was all caught by the TV cameras. "He was in front of me, shouting and trying to block my way, so I took him out" explained Chrétien. "He was a lightweight probably. I just moved him out." The media soon dubbed this "move" the "Shawiningan handshake" in reference to Chrétien's upbringing in the small Québec town.

Scrappy Jean has always been a tough nut to crack. The 18th of 19 children (only nine of which survived), Chrétien's boyhood nickname was "Ti-Jean," short for "petit Jean," even though he would grow up to be six foot two. He wasn't the best looking boy and suffered from partial facial paralysis caused by Bell's palsy, the result of frostbite when, at age 12, he had to walk from his brother's house to his sister's wedding in frigid February temperatures. Chrétien is also partially deaf in one ear, a problem that dogged him throughout his later career. Once, while at a press conference with U.S. President Bill Clinton, Chrétien was asked by a reporter about the illegal drugs that were entering the U.S. from Canada. The prime minister hadn't heard the question properly and quickly quipped, "It's more trade." While everyone burst out laughing, Chrétien replied, "Drugs?…I heard 'trucks'!"

As a youth, Chrétien hated his boarding school so much that he concocted a scheme to fake appendicitis and go home early. He was so good at the prank that the doctors actually agreed to take out his appendix. Rather than face the music, Jean remained tight lipped and underwent the surgery. While Chrétien may have been a decent actor, he certainly wasn't a very good singer. In 1970, Chrétien escorted the Queen to a plaque dedication in Fort Providence, Northwest Territories. The event was to culminate in a public rendition of "O Canada." At the last minute, the board president backed out saying he couldn't sing, so Chrétien offered to lead. Unfortunately, no one joined in. He began to sing in French and forgot the English version. Chrétien was also out of tune, worse than fingernails on a chalkboard. His wife, Aline, later called it the most embarrassing event of her life. Even Prince Charles, when meeting Chrétien years later, remarked that he hadn't forgotten the name Jean Chrétien since his "rendering of the Canadian anthem has become legend!"

Despite his guffaws, Chrétien was known as a fierce defender of Canadian unity, but the country wasn't the only thing he defended. In 1995, an intruder armed with a knife broke into Jean and Aline's bedroom at 24 Sussex

in the middle of the night. Fortunately, Aline had heard the footsteps, woke Jean and called the police. While waiting for the RCMP, Chrétien grabbed the nearest heavy object to use in self-defence—an Inuit stone carving—until the police arrived, a full seven minutes later. It was pure Chrétien, utterly fearless and definitely out of the ordinary.

## Tastes Like…Tofu!

Jean Chrétien belongs to a select club of politicians who have been officially "pie-ed." Other famously pie-ed Canadians include Ralph Klein, Stéphane Dion, Alan Rock and Bernard Landry, although the former Québec premier dodged the pie, causing it to inadvertently hit two people standing beside him. In 2010, Gail Shea, a Fisheries and Oceans Minister, received a tofu pie in the face by a PETA protestor denouncing the seal hunt. Shea didn't freak out, but a few incensed Members of Parliament said they thought pie-ing should be considered an act of terrorism. The Entartistes—a group of "pie-ers" that began in Belgium and gained members around the world, including Montréal—disagree. They believe that pie-ing politicians gives power back to the people (try saying that five times fast) and "deflates the egos of the powerful." Check out the list of others who have received a cake or pie in the face: Anita Bryant, Sylvester Stallone, Bill Gates and George W. Bush—and yes, it looks good on them.

Pie-ing for comedy and slapstick effect may have even begun in Canada. In 1889, a performer named Thomas "Doc" Kelley was in Newfoundland when he saw a hotel stable boy being chased by a cook with a pie. The pie hit the boy's shirt, but witnesses started to laugh. The incident gave Kelly an idea. He thought a pie in the face might be funnier and be good for his travelling medicine show. Either way, however pie-ing first started, it'll likely never disappear so long as politicians are within throwing distance.

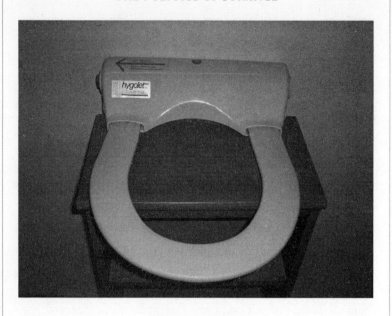

## Toilet Tales

There's nothing like seeing your money go down the toilet. Nova Scotia Premier John Buchanan had a thing against germs, especially the ones on toilet seats. In 1988, he ordered 250 new seats be installed in hospitals and public buildings. But these weren't ordinary toilet seats: they were motorized, high-tech gizmos with a thin plastic seat cover that was automatically replaced after each use. The seats never did get off the ground and were shelved because officials didn't want the public to think AIDS could be transferred from toilet seats (in reality, your average office worker's desk has hundreds of times more bacteria than a toilet seat). Further scandal erupted when a former civil servant testified, among other things, that Buchanan had bought the seats from a friend of his. The province spent thousands more dollars to have the seats shipped to Ontario for an auction. Buchanan later resigned but eventually found a new throne to sit on when he was appointed to the Senate.

# Never Trust a Politician

It was a glaring typo for the editors of the English-language *South China Morning Post*. In November 1995, a photograph of Lucien Bouchard and his wife, Audrey, was mistakenly identified as being of a British couple suspected to be serial killers. The Québec separatist leader and his wife were pictured along with an article under the headline, "Cheerful, Charming Odd-Job Man Driven by Sex and Sadism."

## Looking Like a Dork

They say that image is everything when it comes to politics. Bloc Québecois leader Gilles Duceppe learned that lesson the hard way during the 1997 federal election. Duceppe visited a cheese factory and, for the tour, donned a hairnet as required. Trouble was, he looked like he was wearing a shower cap. Political pundits and editorial cartoonists had a field day with it. Duceppe later fired his campaign manager and media coordinator.

# Pants on the Ground

Usually, debates in Parliament are about as interesting as watching paint dry. One member speaks, a member of the opposition responds, then the original member responds. It's all rather boring and predictable. One dreary day in early 2010, New Brunswick Liberal provincial legislature member T.J. Burke decided to add a little levity to the floor. After opposition leader David Alward made comments on the government's plan to sell New Brunswick's power assets to Hydro Québec, Burke suggested that Alward was caught with "his pants down" and broke out in song: "Pants on the ground, pants on the ground, lookin' like a fool with yo' pants on the ground!"

Whoa! Them ain't just fighting words—they're "General" Larry Platt's! The 62-year-old Atlanta resident sang the lyrics during an audition on the *American Idol* television show. He wanted to make a statement about young men's sagging pant style. The rap medley became a hit with millions of views on YouTube. Even Vikings quarterback Brett Favre chanted the lyrics in the locker room after they beat the Dallas Cowboys in the playoffs. Idol judge Simon Cowell commented that he had a "horrible feeling that song could be a hit." Little did Cowell know that it would end up in the Canadian provincial government. Burke's version of "Pants on the Ground" was broadcast around the world, but thankfully, Burke said he has no plans to start a singing career.

## Warm and Fuzzy Feeling

In 2010, the Canadian Taxpayers Federation gave out its annual "Teddy Waste Awards." The prize for municipal waste went to the City of Toronto. Canada's biggest city actually hired people for $100 per day to pretend they were homeless and count the number of homeless people on the city's streets. Those who were truly homeless, and who probably could have used that paycheque, were not hired for the work. Honourable mention for the Federal Award went to officials who mistakenly sold antique silver from the Governor General's residence for $4000 and then spent almost $100,000 to get it back.

# STANDING ON GUARD, MOST OF THE TIME

*There's no doubt we're proud of our Canadian military, and we've got the history to prove it. Dig a little deeper, however, and you'll run across some oddball occurrences and surprising decision-making over the decades. From a secret spy school to a Canadian-made UFO, we've raised a few eyebrows, including our own. Fast forward to more recent events, like 9/11, and life can get downright weird. Maybe it's a sign of the times, and strange times are here to stay. No worries, we've got Canada's military to protect us, right? Well, if that doesn't reassure you, just remember Canada does have a secret weapon—the Eh-bomb.*

## "Kurt," the Nazi Weather Station

The Atlantic was full of German submarines, or U-boats, during World War II, but they relied heavily on accurate weather reports. To collect data such as temperature, wind direction and so on, and seeing as weather patterns move from west to east, the Nazis realized they needed weather stations as close to the action as possible. They devised several battery-operated stations that could relay information by shortwave, including one named "Kurt." A U-boat set up "Kurt" in Martin Bay, Labrador, in 1943 under a fake sign indicating it was the property of the "Canadian Weather Service." The Nazis even left a few empty American cigarette packages on the ground so it looked like the Allies really had set up the station. Reports are sketchy as to whether or not "Kurt" actually worked after the first few weeks, but the Allies never did intercept any signals. After the war, "Kurt" was forgotten until 1981 when a retired engineer interested in history, with the help of the Canadian Coast Guard, located the remains of "Kurt" and subsequently put them on display at the Canadian War Museum in Ottawa.

### Bomb Saskatchewan

Toward the end of World War II, the Japanese military released 9000 paper "balloon bombs" over the forests of Canada and the United States. The balloons contained highly explosive bombs and travelled the jet stream over the Pacific until they reached North America three days later. The Japanese hoped the balloon bombs would set off massive wildfires at their destinations. Most were shot down before they could explode, but eight bombs reached Saskatchewan between January and May 1945. No one in Canada was hurt, but one balloon that landed in Oregon killed six people and another knocked out power at an atomic research plant in Washington State. Ironically, this was the same plant involved in the production of plutonium used for the atomic bomb that was dropped on Nagasaki on August 9, 1945.

 It was June 20, 1942, and Canada was under attack. Approximately 30 rounds of shells from a Japanese submarine hit the Estevan Point lighthouse on Vancouver Island, the first time an enemy had fired on Canadian soil since the last century.

## The Price of Medals

It took John McCrae only about 20 minutes to pen his famous "In Flanders Fields" poem outside a cemetery near Ypres, France. Not thinking it was very good, he actually threw it away, but luckily, another officer found it and sent it to the newspapers. It was first published in *Punch* on December 8, 1915. McCrae later died in battle, but his poem became a symbol of Canada's war veterans. In 1977, McCrae's war medals were to be auctioned off, but the War Museum and other Canadian establishments said they couldn't afford the $20,000 price tag. It was a Toronto businessman named Arthur Lee who bought them for about half a million dollars and donated them to McCrae Museum in Guelph.

# COLD WAR ZANINESS

## The Canadian Candidates

*I don't even know what street Canada is on.*

–Al Capone, American gangster

In 1951, Canadian and British officials secretly met with members of the Central Intelligence Agency (CIA) at the Ritz-Carlton Hotel in Montréal. They were there to discuss, of all things, brainwashing and de-programming. Funds were distributed to researchers, including Canadian psychiatrists, who performed secret mind control experiments at the Royal Victoria Hospital between 1951 and 1954. These included sensory deprivation, sleep induction and the administration of drugs such as LSD, among other scary treatments designed to wipe the memories of patients. Years later, the Canadian government was ordered to pay millions in compensation to 80 unfortunate patients.

### Operation Lifesaver

It was to be an unprecedented civil defence exercise involving 40,000 Calgarians but turned out less massive and less exciting than expected. In 1955, plans were announced for a practice mass evacuation of Calgary, in which thousands of residents would have two hours to get to the "safety" of surrounding towns. The event was so exceptional that even NATO and Vancouver said they'd send observers. Organizers planned every minute detail for the exercise, which was to take place on the morning of September 21. What organizers didn't plan for was the crummy weather. The temperature dropped to 3°C, and snow made the roads treacherous. The event was called off, and a new date a week later was chosen. At 10:50 AM, the sirens went off again along with a few special effect "smoke bombs." While a number of would-be participants complained they couldn't get that day off work, hundreds of others piled into their cars and left as planned.

Curiously, the safe towns later said fewer "evacuees" arrived than anticipated. For example, 3500 were expected in Innisfail but less than 400 showed up. The numbers weren't much better in other towns such as Strathmore. Perhaps many would-be participants couldn't leave work a second time. Perhaps it was the intermittent rain showers. Or perhaps many *did* get the day off and enjoyed a little "staycation" instead.

## Camp X: The Secret Spy School

Drive along the 401 highway east of Toronto, between Oshawa and Whitby, then down a side road toward a large liquor warehouse. A few steps behind the booze building, you'll see a green park-like area with a sign indicating "Intrepid Park." It reads:

### *Camp X 1941–1946*

*On this site British Security Coordination operated Special Training School No. 103 and Hydra. STS 103 trained allied agents in the techniques of secret warfare for the Special Operations Executive (SOE) Branch of the British Intelligence Service. Hydra network communicated vital messages between Canada, the United States and Britain. This commemoration is dedicated to the service of the men and women who took part in these operations.*

Agents? Intelligence Service? Secret warfare? Unassuming Canada was once home to the first training school for secret agents in North America. Officially, it was called "Special Training School No. 103," but later it became known as "Camp X." The school was set up by the British on 260 acres of farmland and run by Canadian William Stephenson of Winnipeg, a decorated World War I flying ace (and the subject of the famous book, *A Man Called Intrepid*). Stephenson may have also been the inspiration behind the "M" character created by James Bond writer, Ian Fleming. Fleming most likely didn't attend Camp X, but Roald Dahl, the *Charlie and the Chocolate Factory* author, did when

This monument at Intrepid Park is all that remains of Camp X.

he worked for the British Information Service during World War II.

For almost five years, Camp X was a busy training facility where some 500 trainees were taught espionage, counter-intelligence and essentially everything the British knew about secret warfare. Many recruits failed, but others went on to use their skills in various parts of the world. Camp X was also home to a large radio transmitter called HYDRA. In the days before the CIA, the HYDRA communications network relayed material between London and Washington. In 1945, famed Russian defector Igor Gouzenko secretly stayed at Camp X. Gouzenko had worked at the Soviet embassy in Ottawa but defected in 1945 after producing documents that showed proof of Soviet spying as well as plans by Stalin to steal nuclear secrets. Gouzenko later became an award-winning writer and often appeared on television, his face covered by a paper bag. With the end of World War II, Camp X was decommissioned, and the buildings were finally demolished in 1969. Nothing remains of Canada's secret spy school except Intrepid Park, the monument and the intrigue.

# Shh…the Diefenbunker is Supposed to Be a Secret

In 1959, the Canadian government started to build what it dubbed Project EASE, or the Experimental Army Signals Establishment, near the town of Carp, west of Ottawa. But when a curious journalist noticed boxes containing 78 toilets outside the construction site, he knew this wasn't a building for only 150 men. The structure was actually an underground secret defence facility designed to withstand a nuclear blast. The "Diefenbunker," named after then Prime Minister John Diefenbaker, covered 100,000 square feet and was the equivalent of a four-storey office building, complete with a hospital, bedrooms, kitchen, radio studio and even a Bank of Canada vault. In the event of a nuclear war, up to 350 officials could presumably keep the government working—at least for a month, anyway. The Diefenbunker was finally decommissioned in 1994 when the Canadian Forces Station in Carp closed down. Today, it's a National Historic Site where 25,000 people a year visit for a guided tour.

## Take Me to Your Prime Minister

Back in the 1950s, people were either chilled out by the Cold War or that other enigmatic threat, flying saucers. The British were close to developing a saucer-shaped fighter, but it was in Canada where the Avrocar, a disk-shaped craft, took off—well, sort of. In Malton, near Toronto, design engineer John Frost and his team had been working on a circular fighter aircraft with vertical take-off and landing (VTOL) capability. Despite tight security, the secret was out in 1953, and the Minister of Defence confirmed in the House of Commons that Avro-Canada, a subsidiary of the British Avro firm (yes, the same company that worked on the ultimately doomed Avro Arrow jet fighter) was building its own "mock-up model" of a flying saucer.

When the Canadian government ran out of money, the United States Air Force contracted Avro for the VZ-9-AV, or Avrocar. This "flying jeep" would supposedly replace helicopters; there were even hopes for a passenger craft, the Avrowagon; an air ambulance, the Avroangel; and a similar vehicle for sea rescues, the Avropelican. In 1959, the Avrocar was ready for test flights. The craft had a special "turbo-rotor," a type of large fan in the middle that sucked in air and expelled it out the edges. Unfortunately, it couldn't fly more than a couple of feet off the ground and ended up looking like a wobbly Frisbee. In 1961, after spending $7.5 million on the project, the U.S. pulled the plug. Frost eventually moved to New Zealand, and Canada never did build another flying saucer—at least that's the official story.

# STRANGE SKIES

## Gander and the Plane People

When the World Trade Center and Pentagon were attacked on September 11, 2001, all civilian aircraft in North American skies were immediately ordered to land at the nearest airports. At Halifax International Airport, planes were literally lined up on the runway, filled with over 12,000 stranded passengers. For dozens of transatlantic flights, the closest airport was in Gander, Newfoundland. Of the 40,000 international passengers diverted to Canadian airports, 6600 arrived in Gander, almost doubling the town's population. Assisted by the Red Cross, school buses took passengers, sans luggage, to community centres, gymnasiums and halls that had been temporarily converted into mass lodging areas. Locals opened up their homes to give the unexpected visitors, the "plane people" as they were called, whatever they needed. When airspace reopened a few days later, the impromptu hosts were not soon forgotten. Grateful passengers set up a scholarship fund for Gander youth, and Lufthansa airlines even renamed one of its aircraft *Gander Halifax* to thank the cities for their hospitality.

### We're All Grounded

Canadian skies may have been devoid of planes on September 11, 2001, but it wasn't the first time—it was actually the fourth. The first occurred, coincidentally, also in the second week of September, but in 1960. Operation Sky Shield, an exercise by the North American Air Defence Command (NORAD) closed the skies between 1:00 AM and 7:00 AM to test their continental defences against a possible Soviet attack. It was a huge drill involving over 250,000 military personnel from Canada, the U.S. and the United Kingdom. The second instance occurred on October 14, 1961, when Operation Sky Shield II was activated for 12 hours. Select airports in the U.S. took advantage of the no-fly time to give tours of their facilities, while bombers from Britain pretended they were Russian and tried to enter North American airspace. As it turned out, they flew in too far under the radar, so another drill had to be held on September 2, 1962, between 1:00 PM and 6:30 PM. Operation Sky Shield III was a test in which military jets posed as civilian aircraft that were being forced to land under a simulated attack. It was an aerial exercise that never had to be implemented… until 2001.

# No Controversial Authors Allowed

In the days before 9/11, the CIA warned aviation authorities of a possible terrorist attack by Islamic extremists. Author Salman Rushdie had been the target of death threats by fundamentalist Iranian clerics since first publishing his controversial book, *The Satanic Verses,* in 1988. One of the airlines that refused to let him fly during the 9/11 furor was Air Canada. They explained to him that the security it would require just to protect him might cause long delays for other passengers, but the airline later reversed its decision and permitted him on board the aircraft. Wouldn't you want to be the lucky guy who got to sit next to Mr. Rushdie on that flight? Realistically, though, all that extra security would make it the safest airplane ride you'd ever take!

## Buzz the Prez, RED ALERT!

Mere hours before U.S. President Barack Obama's first state visit to Ottawa in February 2009, Canadian F-18 fighter jets intercepted two incoming Russian bombers. While the Russian planes didn't exactly enter Canadian airspace (they were about 190 kilometres northeast of Tuktoyaktuk) they were close enough to give Prime Minister Stephen Harper the chance to jump on the "true North strong and free" bandwagon. "Yes," admitted his Minister of Defence, Peter MacKay, "F-18 jets were scrambled from NORAD in Canadian Command." He went on to add that the Canadian pilots sent a "clear message" for the Russians to turn around

and get back into their own airspace. While answering media questions, MacKay warned Russia to "back off" from Canadian airspace and to not repeat the mistake—fighting words almost strong enough to rekindle a little Cold War sentiment. Moscow quickly shot back, saying their planes did nothing wrong and that MacKay's response was "a farce." MacKay replied that similar incidents had happened before, and he stressed the "importance of NORAD...and exercising our sovereignty." So there!

# WHAT LANGUAGE DO YOU SPEAK?

*A Canadian is one who knows how to make love in a canoe.*

—Pierre Berton, Canadian non-fiction author

*Well, that's one definition…but I, for one, wouldn't know. What I do know is that we Canadians often take part in some curious, outlandish and madcap activities. From twisting the wrappers of chewing gum into ropes to watching our clown in space, it's wild, it's extreme and it's totally Canadian. As for Pierre Berton's description of what Canadians are capable of, is that with or without a life vest on?*

## Crazy Talk

Do you speak Canadian? It's not a simple "zee" versus "zed" situation. If you've ever told someone you want to buy a "two-four" or have used the expressions "Bob's your uncle" or "I'm browned off," then yes, you'll be talking in tongues to anyone outside our borders. Here are some uniquely Canadian words and terms guaranteed to stump foreigners:

*Bangbelly:* a Newfoundland dessert made of molasses, flour, raisins and salt pork

*Bunny hug:* a hoodie sweater

*Click:* a kilometre, as in "go 20 clicks down the highway"

*Dainties:* little cookies and squares

*Deke:* a short version of the word "decoy," first used as a hockey term for stickhandling the puck

*Dépanneur:* this French word actually means a road mechanic, but now refers to any type of convenience store, such as the chain *Couche-Tard* (the one with the sleepy owl sign)

*Gotch/Gitch/Gonch:* men's underwear

*Jambuster:* a jelly donut

*Keener:* slang for an eager student; a brown-noser

*May two-four:* Victoria Day holiday weekend around May 24, while "two-four" is also slang for a flat of beer (which has 24 bottles or cans)

*Moose pasture:* a worthless piece of land or a bog, as in "you were sold an acre of moose pasture"

*Muskeg:* from the Cree word meaning "bog," and we've got more than a million square kilometres of it, more than any other country (no wonder moose love living in Canada so much!)

*Parkade:* a parking garage

*Pogo:* you would order a "corndog" in the U.S., but here in Canada, it's also called a pogo (after the popular brand)

*Scrum:* Canadians use this rugby term to describe reporters crowding around a politician

*Shebang:* slang for "everything," as in "the whole shebang"

*Statutory holiday:* a legal or bank holiday day off

**Question:** *How do you spell Canada?*
**Answer:** *CEE, eh?, EN, eh? DEE, eh?*

*Tuktusiuriagaticitqingnapinngitkyptinnga* is one of the longest words in the Inuvialuktun dialect and means, "You'll never go caribou hunting with me again."

# Land of the CN Tower of Babel

You can tour the world without leaving the Greater Toronto Area. With 110 languages and dialects spoken among its 2.5 million inhabitants, it's definitely one of the most ethnically diverse cities on the planet. And if you thought having two official languages—English and French—was a challenge, try translating in the Northwest Territories. They have 11, count 'em, 11 official languages: English, French, Chipewyan, Cree, Gwich'in, Inuktitut, Innuinnaqtun, Inuvialuktun, North Slavey, South Slavey and Dogrib.

## No Apostrophe "S" Allowed

Language problems have been especially sensitive in Québec. In 1977, Bill 101—the French Language Charter—was enacted by the province to preserve the French linguistic culture and make it the official language of Québec. One notable complaint by Charter enforcers was the apostrophe "s" in Schwartz's, the famous Montréal delicatessen that had been in business since 1930. The new law required that Schwartz's remove the apostrophe as only French language signs were permitted. The cross-Canada department store, Eaton's, as well as Simpson's and others, had the same problem. Eventually, Eaton's changed to Eaton only in Québec, and Schwartz's was allowed to keep its apostrophe "s" so long as it added "Charcuterie Hébraïque de Montréal" on its sign.

# Chat in Gaelic

Want to study the ancient language of Gaelic? You can do so in Cape Breton, Nova Scotia. Although far fewer residents speak it now than a century ago, that's slowly changing. Besides the annual Gaelic Festival, Cape Breton has a Gaelic College of Celtic Arts and Crafts, and Saint Francis Xavier University offers Scottish Gaelic studies.

# JUST DO IT

## Grin and Bear It

Human teeth are extremely strong. Just ask boxer Evander Holyfield, who had his opponent Mike Tyson bite off a chunk of his ear during a heated match. If milk makes your bones and teeth even stronger, then maybe Kevin Fast, from Cobourg, Ontario, drinks a lot of milk. In 2009, he set a world record when he pulled an aircraft weighing 188.83 tonnes over eight metres using only his teeth.

### Chew on This

Do you throw away your gum wrappers? Gary Duschl, who was born in Hamilton and raised in Waterdown, Ontario, started his gum wrapper chain back in 1965. In 1995, he broke the Guinness World Record for the longest gum wrapper chain, but he didn't stop there. As of March 2010, the chain contains one and a half million wrappers, or almost 20 kilometres worth. Gary mainly uses Wrigley wrappers for his chain. Check out his website at www.gumwrapper.com.

# That's ONE CRAZY CANUCK!

## One Giant Leap for Clowns

Québecker Guy Laliberté doesn't have a science or engineering background, and his qualifications consist more of busking and fire-eating than academics. Back in the 1980s, Laliberté was touring around as part of the French Canadian street entertainers known as Les Échassiers de Baie-Saint-Paul (the Baie-Saint-Paul Stiltwalkers), but within four years, he had set up his own group, the Cirque du Soleil (Circus of the Sun), just in time for the 450th celebration of Jacques Cartier's discovery of Canada. Headquartered in Montréal, the Cirque now employs a staff of over 1600, many of them former champion gymnasts and athletes. Their intriguing human acrobatic performances have entertained millions across the globe.

So what does the founder of a hugely successful enterprise do with his money? Buy a ticket to space, that's what. In September 2009, Laliberté not only became the first Canadian space tourist but also the first clown in space. The Poetic Social Mission, as Laliberté named the exercise, was part of his effort to increase awareness about clean water access for the poor back on Earth.

## Talk to Me

On February 2, 2009, at 12:29 PM, four Humber College students from Toronto were talking on a ham radio they made in a classroom lab. Sure, people talk on ham radios all the time, but they're not usually talking to the International Space Station, orbiting 400 kilometres above the Earth. Astronaut Sandra Magnus on board picked up the message and replied,

"Hello? I have you a little bit weak, can you try again?"
The students responded and conversed with the astronauts for
10 minutes. Now *that's* a long-distance call!

## Trading Up

To us, it's just a little red paper clip. To Kyle MacDonald of
Montréal, it turned into a house. In July 2005, he went on the
Internet and traded a red paper clip for a fish-shaped pen.
The pen was traded in turn for a funny-looking doorknob,
which in turn he traded for a Coleman stove, and so on, and
so on. He eventually traded an afternoon with Alice Cooper
for a KISS snow globe, which caught the ear of actor and

sometime snow-globe collector, Corbin Bernsen from the
*L.A. Law* television series. Intrigued, Bernsen offered
MacDonald a part in a movie in return for the snow globe.
MacDonald accepted and was surprised when the town of
Kipling, Saskatchewan (population 1100), said they would give
him a house in exchange for the movie role. After one year and
14 trades, MacDonald had his house, and Kipling had its film
fame. In 2007, the town installed a four-metre-high jungle gym
shaped like a red paper clip, and MacDonald later donated the
house back to the town as a tourist attraction.

## Yes, There Is a Santa and He Takes Emails

Every Christmastime, Canada Post receives over one million letters
and tens of thousands of emails to Santa. Some 11,000 volunteers reply on Jolly St. Nick's behalf in 25 different languages,
including Braille. By the way, Santa's postal code is HOH OHO.

### The Gentleman Bandit

He was known as Grey Fox, and he was a polite, gentlemanly
robber who never actually fired a gun when he committed
grand theft. Bill Miner, an American stagecoach robber, was
also believed to have been first to use the phrases "hands up"
and "sorry to have troubled you" during one of Canada's first and
most sensational train robberies. On September 10, 1904, Miner
and two accomplices robbed a CPR train at Silverdale, British
Columbia, just east of Vancouver. He escaped with the equivalent of over $5 million in gold and bonds but was soon back to
his old ways and robbed another train in May 1906. This time,
Grey Fox was apprehended and sentenced to life in a provincial
penitentiary. The stolen money, as well as $300,000 worth of
government bonds, were unaccounted for, but rumours started
circulating that Miner had been offered his freedom in exchange
for the hidden loot. Conveniently, Miner "broke out" of prison
three months later, and the bonds were quickly recovered by the

Canadian Pacific Railway. When word of the escape surfaced, the federal government was not particularly happy about the situation, which Prime Minister Wilfrid Laurier described as a "shock." By then, Miner had already disappeared back into the U.S. only to be recaptured after committing another train robbery. Some people just never learn.

## Who Would Steal That?

Employees at Ripley's Believe It or Not Museum in Niagara Falls, Ontario, were left scratching their heads when they arrived at work one morning in February 2000. Overnight, someone had climbed the fence, smashed a double-locked display case and stolen an unusual artifact. The missing object was reported to be the shrunken head of a South American warrior, acquired in 1926 and worth USD$24,500. It was described as being about the size of a fist, with long dark hair and a very stunned expression.

A shrunken head

### Lord Black Wears Prison Orange

Conrad Black renounced his Canadian citizenship in 2000 to become a British Lord, but the media mogul may have wished he had kept it when he was found guilty in a Chicago courtroom of mail fraud and obstruction of justice in July 2007. Black was forced to pay millions in forfeiture and was sentenced to six and a half years in prison but still insisted he had done nothing wrong. In 2008, Black—or rather, inmate No. 18330-424 of Coleman Federal Prison in Florida—appealed his conviction but was turned down. But Black isn't one to give up or change his ways. Back in his school days, Black and two classmates sold exam answers but were caught when another boy ratted them out. Black was expelled and forced to attend Trinity College School in Port Hope.

 Alvin "Old Creepy" Karpis has spent the most time out of anyone in Alcatraz, and to boot, he's Canadian. Karpis was a burglar and bank robber who actually had his fingerprints surgically removed by an underworld doctor to avoid detection. For 26 years, Karpis was held in the infamous Californian jail until his deportation back to Canada after his release in 1969.

# Human Pincushion

In 2003, a piercer at the Winnipeg tattoo studio pushed 702 18-gauge needles through his skin in just under eight hours. The needles stayed in for just over five minutes before the squirm factor became too much.

Speaking of body piercings (or mutilations, if that's your opinion), one of the most tattooed women in the world is Alberta strip artist Krystyne Kolorful. Her full "suit" of tattoos covers 95 percent of her body and took 10 years to complete.

# IT'S TRADITION

## Go Jump in the Lake

While most of us celebrate the morning after New Year's Eve by reaching for the aspirin bottle, others have more exhilarating ideas. Here's just a few of the craziest traditions that take place on the first day of the New Year worldwide. In Rome, loopy Italians dive off a 17-metre-high bridge into the Tiber River. In Japan, an icy cold bath is thought to bring luck for the coming year. And around the United States and Canada, it's considered *de rigeur* to dunk yourself in local icy waters. Even Canadian troops in Afghanistan have taken the ceremonial jump into a giant tub filled with 3°C water on New Year's Day.

Perhaps the largest gathering of would-be freezers is in Vancouver's English Bay. The Polar Bear Swim Club touts itself as one of the largest and oldest around. It began in 1920 with only 10 participants, and currently, over 2000 participants and nearly twice as many spectators gather for the charitable event. Registration fees and local donations have become part of these "polar swims," as they're called. It helps make the illogical decision of running headlong into frigid water feel a little less useless.

Oakville has the largest group in Ontario, with typically 350 swimmers and thousands of spectators. Even Port Dover, a tiny town on the shores of Lake Erie, can get 100 or so swimmers every year. They often have to break the ice floes to actually find somewhere to "dip." New Year's Day polar swimmers encompass all types and ages; they're not just crazed young men or beer-bellied old-timers out to impress. In Hamilton, Ontario, one participant "enjoyed" his 63rd consecutive swim in Lake Ontario's 2°C water. He'd first indulged in the tradition when he was a mere three years old.

Dippers do have one experience in common: as soon as the adrenaline wears off, they realize that the water is absolutely freezing cold and have likened the feeling to "ripping off a bandage" or "being stabbed with a million needles, all at once." Sounds like fun! If you do decide to take the plunge next January, here are a few tips from those who have weathered the ultimate in crazy swims:

- Don't shave. Seasoned polar swimmers say every bit of hair helps keep you warm. Try to avoid perspiring before the dip as well.

- Wear a bathing cap so the heat doesn't escape from your head. Wearing a wet suit, however, is a big no-no. You'll likely be called a "cheater."

- Run, don't walk, into the frigid water. If you try to go in slowly, odds are you won't make it past your ankles.

- Wear aqua shoes or other foot protection. Those beach pebbles can feel like tortuous mini ice cubes on your naked soles. Frozen sand isn't much better.

- Many people think that wearing a T-shirt or cut-off jeans might help keep them "warmer." One fellow, who ran in wearing a shirt and tie, later admitted that, "Yeah, that didn't work." The key is to wear the skimpiest bathing suit available (hence some eye-popping male thong wear—you've been forewarned). Once you emerge from the frigid water, any extra clothing will freeze on your skin and actually keep you colder.

- Common sense would dictate that you keep your real clothes on until the very last moment, but a few hardy plungers actually believe you should strip down beforehand to "acclimatize" to the cold. Of course, these are also the people who think that making snow angels or having snowball fights half-naked is a good idea.

- Make sure a buddy is waiting on shore with a very large towel or blanket. The bigger, the better, since you'll want to keep every degree of your body heat once you emerge from your frozen-over hell.

- It should go without saying, but *do not* engage in this craziness if you have heart problems or any other serious medical conditions. Those emergency paramedics are there for a reason. Unfortunately for more than one polar bear swimmer, the cold plunge ended up being the last thing that person ever did.

- Last, but not least, try not to stay in the water longer than 10 minutes. Hypothermia can set in quickly, and you definitely want to be around to do this crazy stunt again next year, right?

# Birthday Grease

Birthday boys and girls in China are often served long noodles to symbolize a long life. In Brazil, the celebrant gets a tug on the earlobe for good luck. Here in Canada, we threaten the birthday child with "birthday bumps," also known as a "grab from behind" and "a knee up your butt" for every year you've been alive. In parts of the Maritimes, there's an old Scottish tradition of greasing the birthday child's nose with margarine or butter so bad luck slips away and won't stick. So you'd better watch out for that condiment ambush on your next big day.

## Bikers, Babes and Friday the 13th

Unless you're into motorcycles and leather, you might want to avoid a visit to Port Dover, Ontario, on a Friday the 13th. Perched on the shore of Lake Erie about half an hour south of Brantford, Port Dover is quaint and picturesque. One might even call it a sleepy little burg, except on those days that happen to fall on the 13th of the month and on a Friday. As soon as the sun rises, Port Dover transforms into a mini-Sturgis (the South Dakota city that is home every August to one of the biggest motorcycle rallies in the world), complete with bikes, bare boobs and beer. It all began in the 1980s when a few buddies decided to ride and meet up in the town every Friday the 13th, and the rally now attracts tens of thousands of bikers and spectators.

# Pick Your Festival

For a "different" kind of festival, look no further than your own backyard. If you want it, somewhere in Canada has it:

*Napanee, Ontario:* We need it, and Napanee's got it—manure that is. Anyone want to come to Manurefest?

*Montréal, Québec:* The biggest bicycle festival in the world isn't in China or Indonesia—it's five days of cycling throughout la ville de Montréal.

*Harrison Hot Springs, Harrison Lake, BC:* Every September, amazing sand sculptures are built for the annual World Championship of Sand Sculpture—just be sure to visit before it rains.

*Windsor, Nova Scotia:* The Pumpkin Festival includes a weigh-off and a Pumpkin Regatta, where you can watch several dozen pumpkin boats (both paddled and motorized) compete in a 500-metre race across Lake Pisiquid.

*Edmonton, Alberta:* The annual Deep Freeze Winter Festival every January helps Edmontonians laugh at their bone-chilling weather and get through the winter blahs.

# GOLD FEVER

*Mysterious inscriptions, buried treasure, northern manhunts and curious finds…lots of interesting stuff hits the fan up here, besides snowstorms and bear hunts, that is.*

## Black Gold

North America's first commercial oil well wasn't out west, but rather it was in Oil Springs, then known as Black Creek, near present-day Sarnia, Ontario. The year was 1858, and a Hamilton man named James Miller Williams was digging for water but struck the black gold à la *Beverly Hillbillies*. The oil was shipped by railway back to Hamilton, where it was refined into lamp oil. Within a few years, Oil Springs turned into a boomtown with 400 oil wells and a population of 4000. Today, the village is home to only about 800 residents, but it does have the nifty Oil Museum of Canada. While some oil still flows from the area, it's admittedly only a tiny fraction (okay, only a trickle) compared to what Alberta produces.

## Camels Laden With Gold

There's nothing like gold fever to bring out the craziness in
Canadians. In the late 1850s, rumours of northern gold brought
in fortune seekers and miners from as far away as California.
To gain access to the mines, the Cariboo Wagon Road was built
in 1862 up the Fraser Canyon. It wasn't an easy trek, lugging
supplies along the road. Enter Frank Laumeister, a man with
a brilliant idea. Why not bring the ultimate beast of burden,
the camel, to assist him in his quest for gold? Laumeister enlisted
a few camels for the job and set them to work. The camels,
though, were not happy campers. When they weren't spitting in
anger, they ate anything, including the miner's clothing. They also
smelled atrocious, and their hooves couldn't withstand the rocky
ground. After four miserable months, the experiment came to an
end. Camels were banned from the Wagon Road and let loose
into the wild. They likely didn't survive the winter, and perhaps
somewhere near the Fraser Canyon lies a camel skeleton or two.

# Gold Rush, Ontario Style

Just the name, Eldorado, conjures up images of a golden town, and such was the hope of this Ontario settlement. In 1866, a part-time prospector named Marcus Powell was hunting through a cave on a local's farm and found a golden nugget the size of a butternut squash. Ontario's first gold rush was underway. Gold seekers from as far away as British Columbia came to find their fortune, but most of the gold was buried deep in ore and was difficult to extract from the rock. Within two years, a new refining process was developed, and eight mills sprang up in the town, reigniting the gold fever. Sadly, it wasn't the most profitable business—the amount of gold recovered was too small to justify the expense. The last mill shut down in 1869, and today, only a few neglected mining cabins remain from the glory days of the Canadian Eldorado, now a part of the Township of Madoc.

# NOW THAT'S EERIE

## The Halifax Explosion

A broken window at St. Paul's, the oldest Protestant Church in Canada, is a ghostly reminder of the greatest pre-Hiroshima man-made explosion ever to occur. The infamous Halifax Explosion took place on December 6, 1917, when a munitions ship, the *Mont Blanc*, accidentally collided with the Belgian ship *Imo* in the Halifax harbour. Over 1600 people were killed, 9000 were injured and 25,000 buildings were destroyed. The blast was so great that an anchor from one of the ships was found over three kilometres away.

As for the window, it sustained damage in the silhouetted shape of a man's head and shoulders. Some say it resembled Reverend Jean-Baptiste Moreau, who was an assistant at St. Paul's in the 1750s. Strangely, another munitions explosion took place on July 19, 1945. This one occurred at a naval ammunition storage depot a bit inland from Halifax. There was only one casualty, a worker at the depot, but thousands of worried people spent the night in parks, just in case.

### Curse of the Lost Lemon Mine

If anyone tells you there's gold near the Crowsnest Pass, Alberta, make sure they're not talking about the Lost Lemon Mine. If it is, then do not, and I repeat *do not*, go there. You may end up like Frank Lemon and his unfortunate buddy, Blackjack. The two prospectors came up from Montana in 1870 to search for gold along the North Saskatchewan River. They didn't find much but decided to follow a trail up the High River. Sure enough, their luck changed, and the two struck gold. That night, however, they got into a heated argument, heated enough that Lemon axed poor Blackjack to death. Apparently, Lemon immediately regretted what he had done and panicked. Worse for him, two young Natives had witnessed everything. They ran back to their chief who, knowing how gold drove the white man crazy, put a curse on the site to keep them away. Lemon tried to return for the gold, but flashbacks of his murderous actions drove him crazy. Later, a trapper who was initially hired to bury Blackjack's body returned with extra miners, all eager for gold. He too fell victim to the curse and ended up drinking himself to death. Then, another prospector who had known Lemon and Blackjack decided he could find the mine and make his fortune. Unfortunately, he perished when the cabin he was staying in burned down. Curse or not, no one has ever struck it rich in the elusive Lost Lemon Gold Mine and lived to tell about it. No one.

# UNSOLVED MYSTERIES

## Susanna Buckler's Baffling Story

In December 1735, a ship named the *Baltimore* was found drifting in the harbour of Chebogue, near Yarmouth, Nova Scotia. The abandoned vessel had been stripped of its cargo and showed signs of having been viciously attacked. Blood and guts were everywhere, but curiously, there were no bodies. A shocked survivor was later discovered wandering on shore—a mysterious woman who said she was Susanna Buckler, wife of the ship's owner, Andrew Buckler. According to Susanna, the ship had been overtaken by the Mi'kmaq and all aboard had either perished in the attack or later died of thirst.

Susanna was taken to Annapolis Royal, the colony capital, to speak with officials. Her story sounded odd, but nothing could be done with so little information. Eventually, more information arrived, this time in the form of a letter sent by the *real* Mrs. Buckler in Barbados. As it turned out, the *Baltimore* had been a convict ship laden with prisoners from England and Ireland, including one woman, a Mrs. Mathews. The convicts had somehow escaped and killed Andrew Buckler, leaving "Susanna" behind. By now, "Susanna," or rather Mrs. Mathews, had returned to England and disappeared. The ill-fated *Baltimore* remained in the harbour at Chebogue for the next seven years until it was finally ordered burned.

### The Ongoing Saga of the Bodyless Feet

It's a recurring headline across the world, a peculiar occurrence for which no one has come up with a reasonable explanation. Since 2007, seven human feet, still encased in their running shoes, have washed up on the coastline of southern British Columbia. An eighth one was also found nearby in the state of Washington. All the feet were still in their shoes and socks, and the bones contained no saw or other tool marks.

A young girl made the first discovery—a size 12 Adidas shoe containing a sock with a legless foot in it. Experts soon deduced that the foot was male, but then another unrelated foot-in-a-shoe was found a week later. In February 2008, a third male foot turned up, followed by a fourth, this time a woman's foot, in May. Hikers noticed a fifth shoe floating in water that June. The detached foot in it seemed to belong to the same man whose other foot was found in February. A match to the female foot from May was found in November 2008. The latest foot washed up on October 28, 2009. Of all the feet, only the first one has been identified, belonging to a man presumed to have committed suicide.

So what's up with all the sneakered feet? Could they have come from accident victims, perhaps of a downed aircraft or a natural disaster? Is there a Mafia or gang connection, or maybe a crazed individual who has access to joggers' corpses? Scientists believe the feet may have come off as the body decomposed. Although each foot showed signs of decay, its sneaker offered good protection from the elements and scavengers. Body parts could theoretically survive years in a shoe until the ocean currents washed them ashore. But what happened to the people who used to own them? And why have no severed, gloved hands ever been found? It's a riddle to be solved one step at a time, so for now, police are doing all the legwork they can.

# Manhunt!

Who was the Mad Trapper of the Northwest Territories? Not much is known about the mysterious, muscular man who went by the name, Albert Johnson. He arrived in Fort MacPherson, Northwest Territories, in July 1931 and immediately built his own trapping cabin along the Rat River. When the trapping season began that December, locals noticed that their own traps had been tampered with. As the new guy in town, Johnson became suspect number one. Two RCMP officers set out for his cabin, but when they arrived, Johnson refused to let them in. The Mounties came back later with three extra men as reinforcements. They knocked on the cabin door again, but instead of a warm welcome, they were greeted with shotgun fire. One constable sustained injuries, so the Mounties had no choice but to pile their comrade onto a dog sled and race back to town.

They returned on January 4, this time with more men and some dynamite. The explosion didn't completely demolish the cabin, but it was enough. As the Mounties sifted through the rubble, they were expecting to find the remains of Johnson's body. It was Johnson, however, who found them first. He had taken cover in a hole dug under the cabin and came out shooting. The siege lasted over a day until the Mounties finally retreated. They returned a week later, but by then Johnson had already left. It was the dead of winter and a bone-chilling –50°C. How Johnson survived in such frigid weather was nothing short of miraculous, since he couldn't light a fire or shoot his gun for fear of being discovered.

On January 30, the Mounties finally caught up with Johnson. He shot back, this time killing a constable, and escaped up a cliff as night fell. Although the Mounties had closed off any access to the passes through the mountains, Johnson managed to climb one of the mountains in blizzard conditions when no one could see him. In early February, the Mounties decided to hire a monoplane to find him. Johnson was eventually spotted, and the Mounties closed in on him. In the final gun battle, nine bullets ripped through Johnson's body. The manhunt was over at last. Johnson was found to have $2000 cash on him, but no one, not even a family member, came forward to claim his body. The identity of the mysterious mountain man remains a mystery.

## Treasure Seeking on Oak Island
If there was ever a money pit in Canada, it would be Oak Island. It all began in 1795 when three boys discovered a cut oak tree branch covering a round depression in the ground. Thinking there was something hidden underneath, they began to dig.

At three metres down, they hit flagstone and a strange platform made out of oak logs. After more digging, they uncovered even more logs. Eventually they gave up, but eight years later, the digging recommenced.

This time, treasure seekers hit on more oak log platforms but also noticed that they contained cement mixed with coconut fibres. Those fibres could only be found in the tropics, so they continued digging and, at 27 metres down, a stone engraved with a mysterious, indecipherable inscription was found. The next day, however, the pit was full of water. Pumping it out didn't work; the pit had been ingeniously booby-trapped to become, and stay, waterlogged. After considerable time and money, the search was abandoned for decades. In the mid-1800s, various companies resumed the attempt, and at one point, a man accidentally died when a pump exploded. In 1893, the Oak Island Treasure Company took over, but another man perished when a pulley broke.

The quest nevertheless continued into the 20th century. Tragedy struck again in 1965 when fumes from a gas pump in the pit killed four treasure hunters. Two years later, another treasure-hungry company lowered a remote-controlled under-water camera down a shaft in the pit. They claimed to see two treasure chests, tools and a severed human hand on the video monitors, but they were unable to recover anything. What could the pirates have left as booty? Theories vary from forgotten Spanish riches to curiosities hidden by the Knights Templar. It will cost millions to continue the search, but treasure seekers vow they will one day conquer the pit. Legend has it the treasure will only be found when the last oak tree is gone from the island and seven men have died seeking it. The oak trees are gone, and six men have died. So far, no one has volunteered to become number seven.

# WRITTEN IN STONE

## The Runic Stone

A 400-pound stone kept at the Yarmouth Historical Society certainly has many visitors stumped. Etched on one side are 13 mysterious characters. Some believe the markings are Norse runes, while others think they represent Mycenian, Japanese or Basque inscriptions. The Runic, or Yarmouth, Stone was found in 1812 by Dr. Richard Fletcher in a cove near Yarmouth Harbour. It was moved to a local hotel in 1872 and even toured as an exhibit in Norway and England during the early 20th century. The stone returned to Canada in 1918, where it remains a popular tourist attraction at its present location. Is it further proof of pre–Christopher Columbus contact, or is the rune simply a ruse by a creative chiseller? The debate continues.

### The Sherbrooke Inscriptions

The saga of mysterious stone etchings continues. Two rows of strange characters were found carved on the inside of a large split limestone boulder discovered in a farm field near Sherbrooke, Québec. A nearby museum acquired the stone around 1910, and one archaeologist declared that the writing was an ancient Libyan language dating back to 500 BC. He interpreted the inscription and said it described an expedition that crossed a great sea and reached land at the rock. Other experts disagreed, but so far no one else has been able to decipher the baffling symbols.

## The Ogham Stone

There is a ancient lichen-covered stone southwest of the historic Viking site of L'Anse aux Meadows, Newfoundland, that has strange carvings. While they may be Aboriginal in origin, the markings are remarkably similar to ancient Celtic script found on similar stones in Ireland. Legend has it that the first Irish saint, St. Brendan

the Navigator, crossed the Atlantic in the sixth century and celebrated mass on what he thought was an island. Could it have been
Newfoundland? Tim Severin, a British navigation expert, set out to
prove such a voyage could have been done. He constructed a boat
out of leather and wood similar to the ones described in early
medieval texts and successfully reached Newfoundland in June
1977. While scholars question whether or not Newfoundland's
Ogham Stone is truly Celtic in origin, a medieval trip across the
Atlantic to Canada was certainly a possibility.

## Hammer of Thor Monument

On the north bank of the Payne River, in Ungava, Québec,
stands a strange, T-shaped rock monument. It is over three
metres tall with a crosspiece and capstone, and the archaeologist who discovered it in 1964 thought it had been made by
the Vikings who may have visited the area 1000 years earlier.
Because the structure looked like a hammer, it was named
the "Hammer of Thor," after the Norse god. *Ungava* means
"far away" in Inuktitut, but it obviously wasn't too far away
for the Vikings to visit if they were actually the ones who
erected the "hammer."

# FINDERS AND KEEPERS

## Seeing Stars

If you ever find an astrolabe—one of those ancient navigational instruments that used the stars to track position—Canada might be a little worried that you'll also be seeing dollar signs. In 1867, a boy named Edward Lee found one in Cobden, Ontario. He sold it for 10 bucks to a Captain Cowley. To make a long story short, it ended up in the possession of the New York State Historical Society, and Canada had to pay USD$250,000 to claim it back in 1989. The astrolabe now sits in the Canadian Museum of Civilization in Hull, Québec.

Enter Mr. Mushrow, the lucky Newfoundlander who went scuba diving in 1981 near Port aux Basques. He found a few bowls and dishes as well as coins dated 1638, and also a strange object he later realized was an astrolabe. It was solid brass, 197 millimetres in diameter and weighed just over four kilograms, with markings similar to one found in a 1641 Spanish shipwreck—except *this* astrolabe had a date of 1628 on it. Mushrow informed the RCMP, but they weren't too interested, so he later went on television to tell people about his find. He simply wanted to have the astrolabe named after him and have it put on display in Port aux Basques.

When the Newfoundland government caught wind of the discovery, they immediately demanded that Mushrow hand the astrolabe over in accordance with the Historic Resources Act. Mushrow invited government officials to his home to view the astrolabe, but they in turn warned him he could be charged for diving for artifacts without a permit and for extortion. Shortly after, the RCMP returned with a search warrant to find the astrolabe. They looked everywhere, except the beam in his basement where it was hanging in full view. Finally, Mushrow handed the astrolabe over, but not before he got the Newfoundland government to sign an agreement with him. Mushrow revealed that he had found another astrolabe in 1983, this one etched with the date 1617 along with the maker's name, Adrian Holland. The Newfoundland government eventually agreed to name the artifacts Mushrow Astrolabe I and Mushrow Astrolabe II and to not press any criminal charges. Furthermore, the astrolabes would be put on display at Port aux Basques every summer, just as Mushrow had wanted in the first place.

## The Gimli Glider

Travel north of Winnipeg to the southern part of Lake Winnipeg, and you'll arrive at a 4.6-metre-high fibreglass Viking statue welcoming you to Gimli, Manitoba. You might think "nice town, weird name, strange Viking." Granted, oddly named towns are a dime a dozen in Canada, and the Viking, well, he was made in 1967 for Canada's Centennial, but Gimli happens to have the largest Icelandic population outside of Iceland itself. In the early 1870s, an Icelander named Sigtryggur Johansson arrived in the area and later named the settlement the Republic of New Iceland, or Gimli, after the home of the Norse gods. And every summer, this port town celebrates its Islendingadagurinn Icelandic Festival on the August long weekend. It is probably the longest and most unpronounceable festival name in the whole country.

But Norse heritage aside, Gimli is also known as the site of one of the most incredible events in aviation history. It occurred on July 23, 1983, when a Boeing 767 en route from Montréal to Edmonton was forced to make an emergency landing on the outskirts of Gimli. Why? The $40-million aircraft with 61 passengers onboard had run out of fuel—it had effectively become a 156-tonne glider, the Gimli Glider. When the warning bells went off, the pilots had initially thought it was just a glitch with the new plane's indicator system. When all the gauges went dark and both engines failed, they realized it was actually a fuel problem. That particular Boeing 767 was one of Air Canada's newer aircraft, fitted with metric-only indicators. It required almost 23,000 kilograms of fuel for the non-stop route, but because of miscalculations by the mechanics and crew, it had less than half that amount. They were 12,500 metres over Red Lake in Northern Ontario in a commercial jetliner with no power.

Fortunately, the pilot had flown gliders before and veered the plane toward an abandoned airstrip in Gimli. The site wasn't entirely abandoned as several families were using it for a drag-racing event, but the emergency landing went off without a hitch and all ended well. As for the Gimli Glider, it was retired to the Mojave Desert for parts in 2008, never to glide again.

## The Snow is so Bright, You Gotta Wear Shades

The Canadian Museum of Civilization also holds the world's oldest sunglasses, a walrus ivory pair dated to about 2000 years ago. These "snow goggles," worn by Inuit ancestors, afforded pro-tection against snow blindness and were often carved from bone or wood, or made from leather, with thin slits for viewing.

### Anyone Missing a Shoe?
An ancient Aboriginal moccasin was discovered by two First Nations children of the southwestern Yukon in 2003. Frozen in an ice patch, the artifact was thought to be a hunting bag until it was pieced together over 240 hours. The 1400-year-old moccasin is believed to be the oldest in Canada and was prob-ably worn by the Athapaskan people.

# WEAR IT AND WANT IT

*For a relatively small country (in population anyway),
Canada has produced its fair share of one-of-a-kind
inventors. We all know about Pablum, and about
Banting and Best's discovery of insulin, a noble feat that
has saved countless lives. And then there are those unsung
heroes who we couldn't do without, providing valuable
inventions such as the zipper, the push-up bra and the
beer case with tucked-in handles. These have probably
benefitted humankind in more ways than we can imagine.
We should all be so proud.*

## The Franks Suit

What do mice, fighter pilots and water-filled condoms have in
common? The anti-G suit, of course. During World War II,
Frederick Banting—who helped discover insulin—became
interested in the reasons why many pilots crashed when they
did steep turns due to the extreme G-forces. His colleague,
Dr. Wilbur Rounding Franks of the Banting and Best Research
Institute at the University of Toronto, decided to do some experiments with mice fitted with water-filled condoms, a type of
mini, primitive anti-G suit.

Later, the full-sized Franks suits were made of rubber and cotton
and had pads full of water to keep pressure on the lower limbs.
Franks donned one in May 1940 and tried it out at Camp
Borden near Barrie. The pilot blacked out, but Franks didn't.
The first to wear it was D'Arcy Greig, pilot of a Spitfire at Malton
airport in Toronto, and it was first worn in battle by British
pilots in French North Africa in 1942. Ironically, Sir Frederick
Banting perished in a plane crash in 1941. He was on his way
to Britain to speak about the Franks Flying Suit Mark II.

## The Other Anti-G Suit

Aside from the anti-gravity suit for pilots, a Canadian invented
another anti-G suit, although that's "G" as in "grizzly." In 1984,
20-year-old Troy James Hurtubise was attacked by a grizzly bear.
Rather than suffer from post-traumatic stress for the rest of his
life, Troy decided to take his experience and use it to benefit
others. As a self-described "close-quarter bear researcher," Troy
felt no one should fear the magnificent bear—and what better
protection against grizzlies than an anti-grizzly suit? With rubber,
plastic, chain-mail and titanium alloy, Troy built the Ursus Mark,
a 67-kilogram bear-proof suit. He said he got the idea from
watching *Robocop*, those cheesy films about an indestructible
robot. The suit was put through a battery of tests, including
being chainsawed, pushed off the Niagara Escarpment and run
over by a three-tonne pickup. Director Peter Lynch even produced a 72-minute National Film Board documentary in 1996
called *Project Grizzly*, and in 1998, Troy won an Ig Nobel
Award (a parody of the Nobel Award) for safety engineering.

# Fashionista New France Style

When Swedish botanist, Peter Kalm, travelled to Canada in 1749, he made note of the plants, wildlife, food, customs and society of New France in general. He even, apparently, noticed the fashions women in Montréal were wearing. According to one historian, Kalm wrote that "every day but Sunday, they [Canadian women] wear a little neat jacket and short skirt which hardly reaches halfway down the leg and sometimes not that far." In other words, the first mini-skirts were worn here in Canada in the mid-18th century! Kalm continued by saying that the "heels of their shoes are high and very narrow, and it is surprising how they can walk on them." Some things never change.

## A Zip-up Doo-da

You can thank a Canadian the next time you zip up your parka. Gideon Sundback was president of the Lightning Fastener Company in St. Catharines in 1925. A decade earlier, he was working in the U.S. and devised a "separable fastener" for the Automatic Hook and Eye Company of Meadville, Pennsylvania. The zipper was first used in military clothes, mainly for the pockets, in 1917. By the mid-1930s, it had closed in on the public clothing market.

# TIME KEEPS ON TICKING

> **Question:** *What was James Bond's secret agent number in Newfoundland?*
> **Answer:** *007:30*

## Those Time Zones

There are 24 one-hour time zones, and Canada has a quarter of them. Yes, we have six time zones, count 'em: Pacific, Mountain, Central, Eastern, Atlantic and Newfoundland Standard Time—but hey, we're a big country. Interestingly, China only uses one time zone, but they didn't have Sir Sandford Fleming. Although he was born in Scotland, Fleming immigrated to Canada when he was 18 and worked as an engineer and surveyor. He proposed time zones in 1878 and promoted the idea at the International Meridian Conference in 1884. It took a few decades, but eventually much of the world had adopted time zones. Fleming died in Halifax in 1915 at the age of 88.

### Spring Forward, Fall Back

The concept of "springing forward" an extra hour in an effort to glean more useful daylight hours for work has been around for ages. Benjamin Franklin was said to have suggested it in the 1770s, but it wasn't until after World War I that most of Europe, and later Canada, subscribed to Daylight Savings Time (DST). The switch to DST took effect the first Sunday in April until the last Sunday in October, but U.S. President George W. Bush extended DST hours in 2007. Canada, not wanting to be responsible for huge trade and travel headaches, followed suit. DST is now observed the second Sunday in March until the first Sunday in November and commences at exactly 2:00 AM on those

Sundays, unless you're in Newfoundland and Labrador, where it starts one minute after midnight, local time.

Either way, that extra hour of daylight on October 31 really screws up Halloween. To make matters more complicated, a few areas in Canada don't make the switch, including most of Saskatchewan. Maybe they're the smart ones. While most of us quickly adjust to the time change, the jump ahead one hour isn't without its pitfalls. Research shows a 17 percent increase in traffic accidents on the Monday after the spring time switch. And a new study proves that while the extra hour of daylight may delay the use of artificial light, it doesn't actually save energy as intended since an increased demand for air conditioning offsets any savings. Way to go, George Dubya.

Remember that famous "Last Spike" photograph? The man standing front and centre holding the sledgehammer is none other than Sir Sandford himself, a tireless promoter of the coast-to-coast railway. He also designed Canada's first stamp, the three-penny beaver adhesive postage stamp, in 1851.

## You Snooze, You Lose

One could say William Frost was ahead of his time. In 1921, Frost was the mayor of Orillia, Ontario, a town about 135 kilometres north of Toronto. If the name sounds familiar, it's because his son, Leslie Frost, went on to become the premier of Ontario from 1949 to 1961. But back to William; he earned his nickname, "Daylight Bill," through his efforts to bring Daylight Savings Time to Orillia. He convinced the town council to move to DST on June 22, 1912. More than a few people, however, forgot to move their clocks ahead one hour, causing mass confusion. Workers showed up for work too early or too late, and stores didn't open on time. The town bell rang at six o'clock instead of at seven, throwing schedules off. Even Daylight Bill neglected to change his clock and arrived at church services late, visibly embarrassed. After two weeks of time-keeping mayhem, the town ditched the time change and went back to regular hours. When the rest of Canada adopted DST several years later, however, Orillia was more than ready.

# TALK ABOUT PATENT PROBLEMS

## Pick Up the Phone

Timing is everything when it comes to filing a patent—just ask Alexander Graham Bell. Well, you could have asked him if he were still alive. Bell emigrated from Scotland to Brantford, Ontario, in 1870. He always had an interest in the latest invention, especially the phonograph and sound transference, seeing as his wife, Mabel, was deaf. Bell even asked his doctor for a dead man's ear bones and used a stalk of hay to tinker with the bones to study sound. By 1874, Bell had developed his first practical telephone, a "harmonic telegraph," and uttered his famous "Mr. Watson, come here" phrase in 1875. The next year, he made the first telephone call from Mount Pleasant to Brantford, just over eight kilometres away. Two weeks later came the first long-distance (and thankfully toll-free) call from Brantford to Paris, Ontario, around 12 kilometres away. Bell filed his patent for the telephone in 1876, mere hours before Elisha Gray, a prolific American inventor. As it turned out, Antonio Meucci, an Italian immigrant in New York, was purportedly working on his own telephone back in 1855, but he was unable to pay the $10 fee required to file the patent. A German inventor, Phillipp Reis, declared he created a telephone in 1861, but back then Germany did not have patent laws. Although the Bell Telephone Company began operations in 1880, Bell had to defend his patent over 600 times in court.

Luckily, that didn't stop him from continuing to invent. He experimented with hydrofoils, large human-carrying kites, gas-powered biplanes, the photoelectric cell, the phonograph and even the iron lung. In 1909, Bell said, "Of this you may be sure, the telephone was invented in Canada. It was made in the United States." Strangely, Bell had his own quirks about the telephone. He thought people should answer the phone with "ahoy" rather than "hello." And although he had a telephone at his country home in Nova Scotia, he wasn't too fond of it. "I never use the beast," he declared.

## Radio Fezzie

Do you like to listen to talk radio or music while stuck in gridlock during rush-hour? Then you've got Reginald Fessenden, the world's first disc jockey and unsung Canadian hero, to thank for that. Between 1887 and 1890, Fessenden was an assistant in Thomas Edison's laboratory and told the famous Edison that he could send human speech through the air without wires. Edison replied, "Fezzie, what do you say are man's chances of jumping over the moon? I figure that one is about as likely as the other." But it was Fessenden who later rigged up the first wireless station, sending the first voice transmission in 1900 from Cobb Island near Washington, DC, to his assistant 80 kilometres away, and then sending the first radio broadcast in 1906. He transmitted a portion of Handel's music played on a phonograph, then played a bit of violin and read from the Bible.

With such ground-breaking technology, you would think Fessenden could have easily received funding from the Canadian government. But they said "no" because they had already contracted the project out to Guglielmo Marconi, the American who sent Morse code messages from Signal Hill in St. John's, Newfoundland, to Cornwall, England. It didn't seem to matter to the government that Fessenden could send actual spoken words and not just dots and dashes. Instead, Fessenden received money from two Pittsburgh millionaires and went on to create over 500 inventions, including radio sonar (after he learned of the *Titanic*'s sinking), a turbo-electric drive for ships, the wireless compass and, in 1927, a patent for an early form of television. He even helped to build the first power-generating station at Niagara Falls. By his own accounts, Fessenden did all this while he was struggling monetarily and fighting court battles. Before he died, he wrote that he was "ridiculed by journalists, businessmen and even other scientists," but in the end, he was glad for his inventions. Fessenden was buried in Bermuda in 1932; a memorial to him, written in Egyptian hieroglyphics, states, "I Am Yesterday and I Know Tomorrow." Now *that's* a sweet epigraph.

 In 1874, Canadians Henry Woodward and Mathew Evans invented the electric lightbulb but later sold the patent to Thomas Edison. Too bad they didn't know that, by the 21st century, regular lightbulbs would blasted as not being "energy efficient" enough.

# SNOW TOYS

## Snow Removal Machine

Sick and tired of watching his milk sour because of impassable snow drifts, Arthur Sicard of Montréal took a good, hard look at farm threshing machines and came up with the idea for a snow blower. His prototype had revolving metal parts and a fan, but it sucked up and threw out snow instead of grain. After years of tinkering, Sicard rolled out his hand-built, rotary blower in 1925 and, two years later, sold the first machine to the nearby town of Outremont. Later customers included the Québec Department of Highways and St. Hubert airport.

### Ski-Doo Typo

Know anyone who rides a Ski-Dog? If it weren't for a typing error, you would probably know quite a few. Born near Valcourt, Québec, in 1907, Joseph-Armand Bombardier first tinkered with an *auto-neige*, or "snow-car," in his late teens using a Model-T Ford, a sleigh and an airplane propeller. In 1934, his two-year-old son died of appendicitis, in part because deep snow had made the roads impassable. Bombardier went back to work on his machine, and by the mid-1950s, he had developed what he called the "Ski-Dog" to replace dog sleds. He painted the logo on the hood, but the last "g" looked more like another "o" and people thought it said "Ski-Doo." The machine was patented in 1959, and sales doubled yearly. By the mid-1990s, over two million Ski-Doo's had been built. Bombardier died in 1964, but his company has since produced Lear Jets, Dash series turboprop airliners, subway system cars and, most recently, the Vancouver 2010 Olympic Flame torches.

# ODDS AND ENDS

## Making the Whoopee

Yes, the rubber practical joke was birthed here in central Canada. Similar "sit-on-it" bellow-type gags existed before, but they only produced screeching or whining noises, not the famous natural sound perfected by the Whoopee Cushion. In the early 1930s, workers at the JEM Rubber Company on Dundas Street West in Toronto used rubber scraps to complete an inflated device that expelled air just like, well, you know what. The company's sales reps then offered it to the king of gag gifts, Samuel Sorenson Adams—who owned the S.S. Adams Company, the largest American novelty manufacturer—but he turned it down, calling it too "indelicate."

Instead, the Canadian device made it into the 1931 Johnson Smith Company novelty catalogue. Customers could purchase the toy for 25 cents or a deluxe model made of heavier plastic for $1.25. When Adams found out how popular the Whoopee Cushion was becoming, he put out his own version, the Razzberry Cushion, but it never became a bestseller like the original. Today, you can even buy an electronic Whoopee Cushion, the ultimate for those who desire the latest in flatulence humour technology.

# Free-wheeling

Hamiltonian George J. Klein gave disabled veterans a leg up
when he developed the first battery-powered wheelchair, complete with joystick control. But that wasn't the design engineer's
only contribution. He also helped invent the National Research
Council's first wind tunnels, a medical suturing device, the
Weasel snowmobile, specialized aircraft skis and a gearing system
for the famous Canadarm used by NASA on the Space Shuttle.
Give this guy a medal, seriously.

### The Ookpik Craze

A cute Canadian mascot took North America by storm when
it debuted at an American trade show in 1963. *Ookpik*, which
means "snowy owl" in Inuktitut, was a stuffed owl-like sculpture made by an Inuit woman for the show's Canadian display.
With its large, round eyes and huggable form, thousands of
orders poured in for the adorable, albeit somewhat silly-looking
creature. Back then, everybody wanted an Ookpik, although the
fad won't likely be repeated anytime soon. Ookpik may have
been charming, but he was made out of sealskin.

# The Canadian Edison Cooks

Known as the "Canadian Edison," Thomas Ahearn was a natural
when it came to the latest technologies. In 1877, he rigged up
Ottawa's first long-distance telephone call, albeit without permission. He also brought the first street lamps and electric street-
cars to Ottawa, and he invented the electric car heater in 1890
(Yes! Thank you!). Perhaps his best invention was the electric oven,
and in 1892, he was first to cook an entire meal electrically.
The banquet took place at Ottawa's Windsor Hotel and included,
among other delicacies, "Saginaw Trout with Potato Croquettes
and Sauce" as well as "Strawberry Puffs."

## Travel in Comfort

Henry Ruttan of Cobourg, Ontario, invented the first type of air conditioning for railway travel in 1858. He made air flow through a ventilating cap over a tank of cold water on the top of a railway carriage, which in turn cooled the passenger area. Henry got the idea after being stuck in a carriage on a hot summer day. Nothing like baking in the sun to get the creative juices flowing.

# Even the (Stainless Steel) Kitchen Sink

Kitchen sinks used to be made of enamel-coated cast iron. Functional, yes; easy to clean, certainly not. Enter Harry Galley (of all names) from Arundel, Québec. The salesman from the large nickel company, INCO, made a stainless steel sink during the 1930s and finally patented it in 1948.

## Dragon's Den

Here's a rundown of several other "why didn't I think of that" ideas:

*Abdominizer:* Invented by chiropractor Dennis Colonello in 1984, this exercise device is still available at garage sales everywhere.

*Ardox (spiral) nail:* Allan B. Dove, a metallurgist at Hamilton's Stelco Steel Company, hit the nail on the head and invented the nifty ardox spiral nail in 1954.

*Caulking gun:* In 1894, Theodore Witte watched his baker decorate cakes and came up with a puttying tool to insulate windows—the first caulking gun.

*CPR mannequin:* Dianne Croteau invented ACTAR 911, a Cardio-Pulmonary Resuscitation practice dummy, in 1989.

*Crash-position indicator,* or *CPI:* Invented in 1957, the CPI was developed by Harry Stevinson to locate crashed planes.

*Cyberspace:* This term was first coined in the early-1980s science fiction work of writer William Gibson, an American who immigrated to Canada in 1968.

*Electric organ:* The first electric organ was patented by Morse Robb of Belleville, Ontario, in 1928.

*Fog horn:* Developed in 1853 by Robert Foulis, a land surveyor in New Brunswick, the fog horn warns ships with its coded steam whistles, which sound like a teakettle on a megaphone.

*Ginger ale:* The "Champagne of Ginger Ales" was concocted by John J. McLaughlin in 1904. The Governor General liked Canada Dry so much that he granted permission to use the crown and shield on the label.

*Green garbage bag:* Initially created in 1950 by Harry Wasylyk and Larry Hansen for commercial use, it is now part of a weekly chore for men.

*Harlequin Enterprises:* Did you know that the publisher of these bestselling romances is a Canadian company? Who says you can't find love in a cold climate?

*Instant mashed potatoes:* While working for the Department of Agriculture, Edward Asselbergs came up with one of the greatest breakthroughs in "just add water" food—instant mashed potatoes.

*Instant replay:* Television sports just wouldn't be the same without the instant replay, developed in 1955 by CBC's *Hockey Night in Canada*.

*Jolly Jumper:* Parents are forever grateful to Olivia Poole from British Columbia, who invented this useful baby bouncer in 1959.

*Lawn sprinkler:* This was among the many patents issued to African Canadian Elijah McCoy, a.k.a. the "Real McCoy."

*Long-lasting alkaline batteries:* The Energizer Bunny would probably stop "going and going" if Lewis Urry hadn't invented alkaline batteries in 1959.

*Muskol:* Naturally, a Canadian—Charles Coll of Nova Scotia—developed this powerful mosquito repellent; in the beginning, his face graced the product's packaging label.

*Paint roller:* Painting jobs everywhere are easier thanks to this invention by Norman Breakey of Toronto in 1940.

*Processed cheese:* Macaroni and cheese aficionados probably know this one already—processed cheese was created and patented by none other than James Lee Kraft of the J.L. Kraft Company in 1916.

*Push-up bra:* Louise Poirier, a designer working for a lingerie company in Montréal, invented the first Push-up Plunge bra in 1963. It lifts, enhances and generally helps women everywhere defy gravity.

*Road lines:* Those painted lines on the road were the bright idea of J.D. Millar, an engineer at the Ontario Department of Transport in 1930. How did we ever manage without them?

*Robertson screwdriver:* Milton, Ontario, resident Peter L. Robertson created the Robertson (square-headed) screwdriver, proving once and for all that Canadians can bolt, screw or use nuts just like everybody else.

And last, but definitely not least….

*Push-in beer handle:* Invented by Steve Pasjack in 1957, this simple but oh-so-important invention is the perfect solution for carrying that flat of two-four.

> **Question:** *What can we Canadians do if our country is flooded?*
> **Answer:** *Drink Canada Dry.*

# IN THE EXTREME

*Heat waves, cold snaps, ice storms, hail storms, swelter-ing humidity and shivering wind chills—we've seen it all. Pile on avalanches, landslides, hurricanes, floods, tsunamis, tornados and earthquakes, and don't forget the latest volcanic eruption was only 150 years ago. When it comes to weird weather, this country certainly goes to the max, with thankfully more than a few pleasant days in between, of course. No wonder the 24-hour weather channel is so popular.*

## Today's Forecast: Cold Enough for Hell to Freeze Over

If global warming is for real, then why are so many Canadians still freezing their butts off every winter? Does another Ice Age cometh? While scientists point to rising average temperatures over the last few decades, it's those changing weather patterns that are really throwing northern countries like us into a tizzy. According to Environment Canada, the seasons across Canada were "out of whack" in 2009. Take Alberta, for instance. After a balmy November, the temperature in Alberta absolutely plunged, breaking records for extreme cold. On December 13, 2009, it was –46.1°C in Edmonton, literally the coldest city on the North American continent and second only to Siberia *in the world*—and that was *without* the wind chill factor! Take off another –10°C for that, though once your fingers have fallen off as a result of frostbite, who can count?

### How Low Can You Go?

The mercury plummeted to –63°C in Snag, Yukon, on February 3, 1947. While the Great White North is used to chilling out, Yellowknife, Northwest Territories, is, on average, Canada's coldest city. Winnipeg, however, is the *world's* coldest city with a population of more than 600,000 people. Ottawa is the second coldest national capital in the world—the first is Ulan Bator, Mongolia, in case you were wondering.

## If You Can't Stand the Heat, Get Out of Kamloops

With an average temperature of 27.2°C in the summer months, Kamloops, BC, has the hottest summers in Canada. The highest recorded temperature for a Canadian city was on July 5, 1937, when Midale and Yellowgrass, Saskatchewan, baked in 45°C weather. Windsor, Ontario, reigns as the most humid city and the one with the most thunderstorms.

### Sunny Days, or Not

For sunny days, head to Medicine Hat, Alberta, which averages 2513 hours of sunshine every year. If you're a vampire, however, you may want to move to Prince Rupert, BC—it only gets about 225 sunny days per year, or 1229 hours of sunshine. Then again, St. John's, Newfoundland, is the foggiest (and windiest) city in Canada, which makes it particularly attractive for those scare-you-to-death nights.

# Snowmaggedon Land

Victoria, BC, wins the prize as the Canadian city with the least annual amount of snowfall (44 centimetres) while Gander, Newfoundland, shovels out under the most (443 centimetres). At least they can enjoy some killer snowball fights.

Windsor, Ontario, is situated at 42° 18' N, which technically places it south of Detroit (42° 23' N).

# SNOW, THE OTHER FOUR-LETTER WORD

*They say Canada has two seasons: six months of winter and six months of bad snowmobiling conditions.*

## White-stuff Wonders

According to Environment Canada, a septillion snowflakes fall on Canada every year. Just imagine: that's a one followed by 24 zeros. Many of these flakes call Calgary home—the Stampede City has experienced snowfall in every month of the year, including July and August. The biggest one-day snowfall in any major Canadian city occurred on April 5, 1999, when 68.5 centimetres fell on St. John's, Newfoundland. On December 27, 1996, 65 centimetres, or 300 million tonnes, of wet snow fell on Victoria, BC. But if you really like to see the snow dizzily swirling around you, go to Kenaston, Saskatchewan. This town proudly calls itself the "Blizzard Capital of Canada." If you do visit, keep an eye out for their 5.5-metre fibreglass snowman mascot—if visibility isn't near zero, that is.

## Sending Snow South

A New Brunswick company was paid to export snow to Puerto Rico in November for carnival celebrations. The unusual export travelled almost 3220 kilometres south in large refrigerated containers to where visitors paid $10 to play in the Canadian white stuff.

### Lotsa Little Angels

The record for the most snow angels in a multiple venue took place in London, Ontario, on February 2, 2004. A total of 15,851 students, parents and teachers from 60 schools across the London District Catholic School Board lay down in the snow at exactly 2:00 PM and flapped their arms and legs to create the so-called snow angels.

 In January 1999, the mayor of Toronto, Mel Lastman, called in the Canadian army to help clear snow from the streets after the heaviest one-month snowfall ever fell on the beleaguered city.

## The Great Ice Storm

Hell may have yet to freeze over, but the Great Ice Storm of 1998 was certainly hellish for the millions of people it affected. The storm began around January 4 and pelted Ontario, Québec, parts of the Atlantic provinces and the northeastern U.S. for days. Freezing rain left an icy coating up to eight centimetres thick on everything from streets and vehicles to tree branches and electricity towers. When the storm passed, it left behind an incredible sight. The landscape was now dotted with countless ice-encased sculptures that sparkled like crystals in the sun. It was eerily striking, but also devastating.

The sheer weight of all the heavy ice caused many trees to snap like toothpicks and 120,000 kilometres of power lines to collapse.

Without electricity, millions were left in freezing conditions, and at least 25 people died from hypothermia or carbon monoxide poisoning. Farmers struggled to keep livestock alive in unheated and unventilated barns. Cities such as Ottawa, Montréal and Kingston declared states of emergency. The Canadian Armed Forces were deployed to the hardest hit areas to open roads and assist those needing food and shelter. Hydro crews, including those from other areas of Canada and the U.S., worked around the clock to restore power and effectively rebuild the entire electrical grid. Total damage was estimated at $6 billion, and some businesses, such as Québec's maple syrup industry, took years to recover. Besides generators, there was one other product that sold like hotcakes after the weather event of the decade—the "I survived the Great Ice Storm of 1998" T-shirt.

# WHEN THE WIND WHIPS UP

## Tornado Alleys

On average, between 80 and 100 tornadoes touch down in Canada each year. When it comes to tornadoes, we're second only to the United States. Most Canadian tornadoes occur in the prairie provinces, Ontario and occasionally Québec, but twisters have been reported in British Columbia and even the Northwest Territories. The earliest known tornado in Canada occurred on July 1, 1772. It cleared a track through a forested area in the Niagara Peninsula, which locals then appropriately named Hurricane Road.

Here are some noteworthy, as well as other not-so-well-known, tornado tales:

*June 30, 1912, Regina, Saskatchewan:* The Regina Cyclone, billed as Canada's deadliest tornado, was rated an F4. It demolished hundreds of buildings and killed 28 people.

*July 15, 1946, Sedly, Saskatchewan:* A tornado near Sedly, Saskatchewan, left a cow on its back, stuck in the ground by its horns with its legs still in the air.

*August 7, 1979, Woodstock, Ontario:* Two F4 tornados ran through southwestern Ontario and the town of Woodstock, killing one person and causing millions of dollars worth of damage. Strangely, one pig was found alive but wedged in a tree.

*August 11, 1980, Port Dover, Ontario:* A small tornado quickly ripped off a part of a hamburger stand in this picturesque town on the shores of Lake Erie. A few minutes later, a customer tried to order fries, oblivious to the whipped up deep-fryer grease.

*July 31, 1987, Edmonton, Alberta:* A week-old baby bundled in a blanket was found alive on a road after a deadly tornado hit Edmonton and killed 27 people. The tornado, with winds described as sounding "like a giant vacuum cleaner," blew a dishwasher 30 kilometres away—it landed in a farmer's field.

*August 15, 1997, Owen Sound, Ontario:* When a tornado hit southeast of Owen Sound, two men were flung into a lake 100 metres away. Despite being spun underwater, they survived to tell their tale.

# WATER, WATER, EVERYWHERE

## Grab the Life Vest

Noah's ark would have come in very handy when torrential rains and flooding pelted the Saguenay-Lac Saint Jean area of Québec in mid-July 1996. The floods caused $1 billion worth of damage, and the province's environment minister said the event was because of "rains which only happen once every 10,000 years." It was small solace for the families of the 10 residents who perished in the disaster and the 12,000 who fled their homes. While the Saguenay-Lac Saint Jean flood was unusual, inhabitants near Red River, Manitoba, wonder if every springtime should be called floodtime instead. The region's first major flood was recorded in 1826, but there have been plenty more since then.

## Who Turned Off the Taps?

On March 29, 1848, an ice jam blocked the waterflow over Niagara Falls, reducing the great cascade of water to a mere trickle. About 5000 people came out to see the uncommon sight. Some ventured onto the rocky river bed and found previously hidden objects, such as tools and muskets from the War of 1812. Others thought the event was a sign of the apocalypse and went straight to church to pray. Thirty hours later, the ice jam broke. A few minutes later, the Falls were back to normal.

It wasn't the first, or the last, time Niagara Falls was stopped up by ice blockages. Other incidences occurred in 1909, 1935 and 1947. In 1969, the American Falls were even "shut off" to permit engineers to make repairs. Perhaps the most tragic episode took place on February 4, 1912. Three people were swept to their deaths after an ice bridge at the base of the Falls suddenly broke up. After the Great Ice Bridge Disaster, no one was allowed to legally venture onto the frozen Falls again.

# SHAKIN' ALL OVER

## The Big Ones

Did you know Canada has three or four earthquakes *per day*? That fact should be enough to make you quiver in your boots. Luckily, most of these tremors are so minor that only sensitive seismic equipment can detect them. Of course, the "Big Ones" do still happen. An earthquake estimated to be magnitude 9.0 on the Richter scale shook British Columbia the night of January 26, 1700, and was felt on both sides of the Pacific Ocean. Another quake occurred in Montréal in 1723, damaging hundreds of homes and killing one person. A huge, 8.1-magnitude earthquake was reported off the Queen Charlotte Islands, BC, on August 22, 1949. Just to let you know, geologists list five major Canadian cities as being situated in earthquake-risk zones: Victoria, Vancouver, Ottawa, Montréal and Québec City. In the

early afternoon of June 23, 2010, a rare 5.0 magnitude quake with an epicentre just north of Ottawa rocked central Canada and parts of the U.S. Although the 20-second tremor only caused minor damage, it was enough to rattle businesses, school children, and civil servants alike.

**Canadian Tsunamis**

On November 18, 1929, an earthquake rocked the floor of the Atlantic Ocean over 500 kilometres off the coast of Newfoundland. At approximately 5:00 PM, buildings shook in St. John's, but people didn't think it was an earthquake. It wasn't until three days later when a steamship arrived on the Bruin Peninsula that any severe damage was noticed. The area had been hit hard by a tsunami wave that had arrived 2.5 hours after the earthquake. Homes were swept away, buildings were destroyed and 27 people perished. Another Canadian tsunami occurred on March 27, 1964. Although the 8.5-magnitude earthquake's epicentre was off the coast of Anchorage, Alaska, the wave travelled 720 kilometres per hour until it slammed into Port Alberni, BC, four and a half hours later.

## The Mountain That Walks

Aboriginal peoples near Turtle Mountain knew well enough to avoid what they called the "Mountain That Walks." The town of Frank, Alberta, however, was established to mine for coal in the tremor-filled area. Early in the morning of April 29, 1903, a landslide lasting less than two minutes trapped scores of miners, killed 76 people and injured dozens of others. More than three-quarters of the town was affected. Only 12 bodies were ever recovered, but miraculously a baby was found crying but unscathed on a boulder outside her neighbour's home.

**Lethal Canadian Landslides**
*April 26, 1908, Notre-Dame-de-la-Salette, Québec:* A "quick clay" landslide in this town northeast of Ottawa kills 30 people.

*May 4, 1971, Saint-Jean-Vianney, Québec:* After 31 people die in a landslide, the community is moved to safer ground north of Québec City.

*May 10, 2010, St. Jude, Québec:* A sudden landslide swallows a family home, killing all four occupants, and leaves a massive crater approximately 500,000 square metres wide.

 In 1775, Canada's most historically active volcano, Tseax Cone in British Columbia, erupted and killed 2000 Nisga'a First Nations people.

# LOOK UP, WAY UP

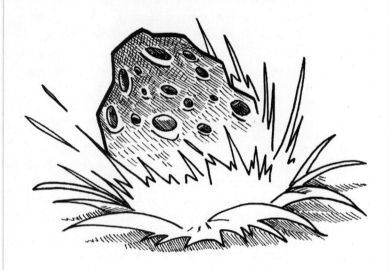

## The Rocks That Fell to Earth

On January 18, 2000, a bright fireball was seen streaking over Tagish Lake, Yukon. Pieces of the meteorite were later found scattered on the frozen lake's surface, and one was recovered by geologists in a "pristine," uncontaminated condition—that is, untouched by bare human hands. In another incident, a black rock that crashed to Earth near a home in Grimsby, Ontario, sat outside the front door for two weeks. The rock had cracked the windshield and dented the side of the homeowners' SUV before breaking into fragments. The owners thought the rock had been thrown by vandals, but when they read media reports of a nearby fireball, it occurred to them that their oddly shaped rock might be a meteorite. It was, and they subsequently loaned it to the University of Western Ontario for study. The Western team even discovered another meteorite not far from the original space rock's landing site.

## Sacred Stone

The Manitou Stone, or Iron Creek Meteorite, is a large, 150-kilogram iron-nickel meteorite originally enshrined on a hilltop near Iron Creek, east of Edmonton. It was revered by Aboriginal peoples as a sacred stone because it came from the sky, and its shape was similar to the profile of a man, perhaps even the Face of Manitou, the Great Spirit. The meteorite was first documented in 1810 and later taken farther north by missionaries. It now sits at the Royal Alberta Museum in Edmonton.

# Lightning Crashes

On April 22, 1932, lightning hit a flock of wild geese over Elgin, Manitoba. The townsfolk couldn't believe it when 52 birds fell straight to the ground—their goose had already been cooked, you could say.

## Runaway Balloon

It's a bird, it's a plane…no, it's a fugitive Canadian weather balloon. Environment Canada and the Canadian Space Agency released a 25-storey-high weather balloon in Saskatchewan on August 24, 1998. The gondola contained $500,000 worth of scientific equipment designed to gather information on the thinning ozone layer. After 24 hours, the balloon was 38 kilometres above the earth and ready to land in Alberta. Remote-controlled explosions were supposed to cut the cable and open a flap that would deflate the balloon. Instead, officials had a "Houston, we have a problem" moment. The balloon didn't sink to the ground as expected, but rather began to drift, and drift, and drift…right toward the North Atlantic. Two CF-18 fighter jets were eventually sent after it. They tried to shoot it down over Labrador, peppering it with 1000 rounds of cannon fire. The balloon briefly lost altitude but refused to descend any farther and even floated through Russian and Norwegian airspace. It finally landed September 2 on Mariehamn Island, Finland, and was shipped back to Canada—by plane.

# HONEY, WHO TURNED OFF THE LIGHTS?

## Lights Out!

Most of us are used to the occasional power-outage during a storm. At 4:13 PM Eastern Standard Time on August 14, 2003, a power-line failure at a generating plant near Cleveland caused 100 power plants in Ontario and the northeastern U.S. to also malfunction. From New York City to Thunder Bay, down the Atlantic coast and as far west as Chicago, approximately 40 million Americans and 10 million Canadians suddenly found themselves left in the dark. It was the largest blackout in North American history. Commuters were stranded on subways, drivers could not pump gas into their vehicles, and office building elevators failed. While most areas affected got power back on the same day, it was enough to shake up a society so wholly dependent on electricity. One group, however, was especially thrilled when the blackout occurred. With no light pollution, astronomers were able to view the clearest night sky in the region since the invention of artificial light.

### Back in the Days of Black and Black

The 2003 Blackout wasn't the first time Canadians wondered why the lights went out. On November 9, 1965, at approximately 5:16 PM, a transmission-line relay failed at the Adam Beck Generating Station in Queenston, Ontario, near Niagara Falls. The power grid across Ontario and the eastern United States went down like a dead duck—the Great Northeast Blackout of 1965 had begun. Approximately 30 million people were in the dark for up to 13 hours. Fast forward to July 23, 1971, when another large blackout occurred, this one over much of Québec. Curiously, there had been a UFO flap around the areas of Rimouski, St. Odile and Sacré Coeur three days earlier.

Witnesses described seeing several red, roundish objects that rotated and pulsated green-and-blue rays. Hmm…coincidence?

## Earth Hour? What Earth Hour?

As part of a global campaign to bring awareness to climate change, one billion people around the world voluntarily turn off their lights for an hour every March 28. The event began in 2007, and even the lights on famous landmarks such as the Eiffel Tower, Sydney Opera House and CN Tower are dimmed while communities hold outdoor festivities such as stargazing or candlelit concerts. Although the goal is to get governments to take more action on global warming, the drop in power consumption during Earth Hour is strikingly noticeable. In 2009, most Canadian cities saw an average six percent reduction in electricity demand—well, except for Calgary. Its power consumption went up 3.6 percent during Earth Hour. Granted, it was very cold in the southern Alberta city that night.

# HMM, THIS REMINDS ME OF...

*Canada only needs to be known, in order to be great.*

–J. Castell Hopkins, Québec historian

*As extreme as Canadian weather can be, Mother Nature has endowed this country with spectacular scenery as well as some very curious sights. Every once in a while, a natural formation occurs that looks so out of the ordinary, or perhaps even lifelike, that it literally freaks us out!*

## Grand-looking Canyons, Canadian Style

If you've got a hankering to see a Grand Canyon but don't want to travel to Arizona, no worries—we have a few right here in Canada. British Columbia, for instance, is home to 80 kilometres of steep-walled canyon in Stikine Provincial Park. After eons of erosion by the Stikine River, the drops can measure as much as 300 metres down, while the width of the unnavigable river varies from 200 metres wide to as narrow as two metres.

Can't make it out west? Try the Ouimet Canyon, a two-kilometre-long gorge northeast of Thunder Bay, Ontario. Still too remote? Join the throngs of tourists and head to Niagara, where you'll find another impressive chasm, the Niagara Gorge. This stunning crevasse extends from the famous Niagara Falls and runs downstream 11 kilometres to the foot of the escarpment at Queenston. The startling greenish-blue hue of the river is the result of erosion, which releases dissolved mineral salts into the water. Oh, and while you're at Niagara, you've only got about 2000 more years to view the American Falls—scientists believe it will have dried up by then. And 50,000 years from now, the Horseshoe Falls will also have eroded away. Tourist bureaus on both sides of the border have been forewarned.

## Mini-desert

No vegetation? Check. Dry climate? Check. Windy with sand dunes? Check. Okay, you guessed it: it's a desert, and you can find it in Canada. The Carcross Desert near Bennett Lake in the Yukon is only 260 hectares, which makes it the world's smallest desert. Thousands of years ago, it was the bottom of a glacial lake. It does get a little precipitation, about 11 centimetres per year, including snow. And in case you're wondering, there are three other semi-arid areas in Canada: the Thompson River Valley west of Kamloops, BC, Osoyoos in BC's Okanagan Valley and the famous Badlands in Alberta.

# I See Senior People

More than a few Canadian natural formations resemble senior men (and thankfully not "mature women"). One is the "Old Man in the Mountain" on Shellbird Island near Corner Brook, Newfoundland. The rocky edge does appear to have the profile of an elderly gentleman. Same goes for the Sleeping Giant, as seen across Lake Superior from Thunder Bay. According to Native tradition, the Sleeping Giant is a Great Spirit who turned to stone, although it does look a little like a snoring grandpa.

## Old Salt

Did you know that more than 500 lakes in Saskatchewan are salty? Like the Dead Sea in Israel, it's easy to float in Little Manitou Lake because it's so salty; in fact, it has more than three times the salt of the ocean. Forget fishing—let's go floating! It's a saline lake, which in scientific terms is an "endorheic" lake that doesn't flow into a river or an ocean. Fed by underground water, it's thought to have healing powers and is a popular tourist destination.

# The Original Freezers

More than a few Canadians probably think the word "pingos" means "cute penguins." Wrong. It would be more accurate to say that the pingo was the original meat locker. Pingos are cone-shaped hills with an icy centre that are formed when the ice under the permafrost layer expands and literally pushes the mound upwards. These odd mounds are found in Russia and other northern freeze-your-butt-off countries, but the world's largest concentration is right here in Canada—we have about 1450 in total—in the Tuktoyaktuk Peninsula of the Northwest Territories. Some pingos are 300 metres in diameter, 50 metres high and over 1000 years old. They're still growing too, about two centimetres every year. Inuit hunters used hollow parts of pingos to preserve meat. They were the perfect freezers: ice-cold, easy to locate and never needing a repairman.

# FREAKY FORMATIONS

## Hoodoos in Drumheller

These sandstone pillars of soft, sedimentary rock are found throughout the Drumheller Valley in Alberta's Badlands. These eerily shaped, top-heavy formations can reach up to seven metres high. Wind and rain erosion have whittled them away over millions of years, while their mushroom-like "caps" protected their shafts.

### Tidal Wars and Flower Pots

The tides in the Bay of Fundy aren't ordinary tides. At more than 16 metres, they claim to be the highest in the world (there is competition, however, as a 2002 tide on Ungava Bay in northern Québec was measured at least one centimetre higher). The Bay of Fundy also contains curious limestone rock formations carved out by the tides to resemble flower pots. Also known as the Hopewell Rocks, you can kayak around these stone pillars then go back hours later when the tide has receded and walk where you kayaked. Off the tip of the Bruce Peninsula near Tobermory, Ontario, stand similar rock formations at Flower Pot Island. There were originally three flower pots, but one fell down in 1903.

## Ontario's Badlands

When tourists flock to Canada's Badlands, they usually mean the ones in Alberta's Drumheller Valley. As for the Cheltenham Badlands in southern Ontario, well, they're not such a tourist mecca. For one, these Badlands aren't very well known, except perhaps to locals. Secondly, they're only 450 million years old, and you won't find any dinosaur bones here. Originally covered in soil and forest, the Cheltenham Badlands were overgrown in vegetation until settlers cut down the trees, farmed and basically let erosion create the strangely barren 37-hectare area. The shale rock has a pottery brown hue reminiscent of the actual Alberta Badlands, and

The Cheltenham Badlands

a nearby town is aptly named Terra Cotta after the local brickmaking heritage. Film crews sometimes use the Cheltenham Badlands for that "alternate planet" background (check it out on a *PSI Factor* television episode or the Our Lady Peace music video, "Starseed"), and it's conveniently situated less than two hours from Hollywood North, also known as Toronto.

## Rock of Ages

There's a geriatric geological battle heating up around Canadian rocks. In 1999, the oldest rock in the world was believed to be the Acasta Gneiss in the Northwest Territories, dated to about 4.03 billion years ago. In 2008, scientists found rocks in a region along the coast of Hudson Bay in northern Québec that may date back to about 4.28 billion years. Not bad considering the Earth was only formed around 300 million years earlier.

# That's ONE CRAZY CANUCK! Grey Owl

Ever wished you could be someone else? As a boy, Archibald Stansfeld Belaney dreamed of escaping his native England for Canada. He wasn't the happiest child, abandoned by his father and left in the care of two strict aunts. When he was 17, Archie finally left his homeland and travelled to Temagami in northern Ontario. Archie felt right at home in the untamed wilderness of the early 20th century. He fought fires, trapped and, for extra income, used his writing talent to pen adventures that he sold to newspapers back in England. He even married an Ojibwa woman named Angele Egwuna, but like his father, Archie didn't turn out to be the best family man. He soon left his wife and their young daughter for a Métis woman, Marie Girard, but ditched her in turn shortly after she became pregnant.

When World War I broke out, Belaney joined the military but suffered a foot injury in a battle. The army sent Archie back to a hospital in England for a toe amputation, and there, he met up with a childhood friend named Florence Holmes. The two quickly married, but before the honeymoon was over, Belaney told Florence the wild woods of Canada were calling him to return. Florence, though, wasn't into roughing it in the bush and refused to go. Undaunted, Belaney simply left England without her.

Back in Canada, he reunited for a short time with his first wife, Angele. He was around just long enough for her to give birth to another daughter before ditching her again. He also learned that he had a son named Johnny with his former spouse, Marie. She had since died from illness, and little Johnny never knew about his real father until he was nine years old. The abandoned son later referred to his uninterested father as "Archie Baloney."

All the while, Belaney was undergoing a type of trans-formation. He grew his hair long and used henna to dye his skin a darker tone. He took the name Grey Owl or, in Ojibwa, He-Who-Flies-By-Night (which was certainly true when it came to relationships). He told everyone he was a Plains Indian from Arizona, with a Scottish father and Apache mother. He boasted that as a child he was a knife thrower in Buffalo Bill's Wild West Show. In 1925, Belaney, or "Grey Owl," fell in love with a young Native woman named Gertrude Bernard, though he preferred calling her by her Iroquois name, Anahareo.

Despite all his secret lies, one thing remained true—Grey Owl was a consummate nature lover. His new wife even turned him into an animal lover. When they came across two orphaned beaver kits, Anahareo convinced Grey Owl to take them home. The baby beavers converted Grey Owl into his new role as a writer and conservationist dedicated to increasing the dangerously low and over-trapped beaver population. The couple moved to Saskatchewan, where Grey Owl wrote and occasionally returned to England for tours. Hundreds of thousands came to hear him and the stories of his beavers, Jelly Roll and Rawhide (the original two had run back into the wild). Grey Owl's books, *Pilgrims of the Wild* and his children's story, *The Adventures of Sajo and her Beaver People,* as well as *Tales of an Empty Cabin*, became bestsellers. Yet once again, he neglected his wife, Anahareo, and their child, Shirley Dawn. She finally left him in 1936, but within a few months, Grey Owl had married Yvonne Perrier.

Shortly after, Grey Owl resumed his tours in England and even met royalty, dressed all the while in full Native costume. It seemed as if the only people who weren't fooled by Grey Owl were the First Nations peoples, who had known him back in Canada. Eventually, a reporter with the *North Bay Nugget* uncovered the truth about Grey Owl, but the editor, fearing Grey Owl's environmental contributions would be tainted, held off running the story. When Grey Owl died of pneumonia two years later at the age of 49, the truth finally came out. The deceased man, known as Grey Owl, had an amputated toe and was actually Archibald Stansfeld Belaney. The paper held nothing back. Headlines of bigamy, fraud and deceit shocked Grey Owl fans for years.

Today, Grey Owl is remembered more for his positive accomplishments than his marital failings. His cabin in Prince Albert National Park remains a popular tourist destination, and visitors can read the thoughtful words etched on a plaque at his gravesite: "Say a silent thank you for the preservation of wilderness areas, for the lives of the creatures who live there and for the people with the foresight to realize this heritage, no matter how."

# In the Middle of Nowhere

How did that enormous rock end up smack dab in the middle of the Prairies? Located near Okotoks, Alberta, the "Big Rock" is the world's largest dumped rock, also known by its more conventional term, an "erratic." Erratics were once carried by glacial ice sheets, but when the glaciers melted some 20,000 years ago, the rocks stayed in place. Prairie erratics are some of the most noticeable, but these oddball rocks can be found in other parts of Canada—one near Trenton, Ontario, is as big as a house and even has a little cave carved into it.

## See You in the Hell Hole

Tell everyone you've been to a hell hole, and there's always someone who won't blink an eye. Early pioneers thought these holes in the forest floor led straight to hell, but modern geologists say they were caused by the surrounding soft limestone, which slowly dissolves in damp weather. Found along certain nature trails in eastern Ontario, hell holes can be as small as rabbit holes or large enough for a person to squeeze through. Some even widen into an underground cave, perfect for that cozy Hades-like feeling.

# TREES, TREES AND MORE TREES

## How Do You Like Them Apples?

Travel along Ontario's 401 highway west of Toronto and don't be surprised if you see a giant apple near the town of Colborne. It's just a roadside fruit market attraction, but the apple is Canada's favourite fruit. An apple tree in front of the National Research Council in Ottawa is said to be a descendant of the famous one that dropped a fruit on Sir Isaac Newton's head. And in 1801, John McIntosh produced the hardy and delicious apple that still bears his name. The original McIntosh apple tree died in 1893, but five trees grafted from it are still growing strong in Dundela, Ontario. Now if only he had known how many computers would bear his "Mac" apple years later.

### Tiny, But Very, Very Old

Some of the oldest trees in Canada are only a few metres high. They are the spindly, small cedars that seem to sprout out of the rock outcrops of the Niagara Escarpment. To date them, their rings must be counted, but you'll need a microscope for that. These trees came from seeds that became lodged in limestone crevices. Although they didn't receive many nutrients, the trees survived and weren't cut down by settlers. Several are estimated to be hundreds, if not thousands, of years old.

## Not Exactly Dead Wood

In the late 1970s, a limber pine in southwestern Alberta passed away. Actually, it remained exactly where it had been for the past several hundred years. Locals knew it was an old tree but left it alone until it fell over during a windstorm in 1998. Instead of hauling the tree away, they propped it back up with rods.

When a vandal cut off one of its branches a few years later, volunteers grabbed a bucket of glue and fixed that too. The Burmis Tree, named after the ghost town nearby, is one of the most photographed trees in the world, and one of the few "rebuilt" ones.

# EXPLAIN THIS

## The 1864 Islands

There's a beautiful region along the western section of the St. Lawrence River called the 1000 Islands. Tourists flock here every summer to boat, picnic and enjoy the pristine waterway. A thousand islands sounds rather impressive, doesn't it? Alas, those glossy tourist brochures can be misleading. I wouldn't call it false advertising, but if you count an island as being a crop of land that is home to at least two trees and is above water every day of the year, then there are actually 1864 islands here. So why don't they call it the 1864 Islands? After all, wouldn't that mean there are more islands to go around, more to enjoy? Perhaps it has something to do with the salad dressing—pass me the Thousand-Eight-Hundred-and-Sixty-Four Islands dressing, please.

### The Teaching Rocks

To the First Nations, the site of the "Teaching Rocks" in Petroglyphs Provincial Park is a sacred space. Often, the scent of burning sweet-grass offerings permeates the air under the modern glass enclosure where the petroglyphs can be seen. It is like entering a church or cathedral; a special place where time seems to stand still. Visitors respectfully gaze on the hundreds of carved symbols etched into a large white rock face and wonder what they might mean. The images depict animals such as turtles, snakes and birds. There are even human figures, perhaps shamans, and others that look eerily alien. Cracks in the rock are thought to be pathways to the underworld.

Petroglyphs are found all over the world but these, located some 55 kilometres northeast of Peterborough, are the largest group of its kind in Canada. They are believed to have been carved by the Algonquin-speaking peoples anywhere from 500 to 1000 years ago.

The site was largely forgotten until 1954, when prospectors published their discovery in a local paper. It took another two decades until the area became a provincial park, but now the carvings are adequately protected from the elements. What do the etchings teach? Some say they show life and how man must coexist with nature. Others point to a rock carving of a curious, narrow boat unlike those of ancient First Nations. Could it describe visitors who arrived centuries before any known explorers? For now, no one knows. Perhaps the lessons the rocks teach are yet to be learned.

## Magnetic Hills

Don't tell the kids, but magnetic hills are not really magnetic—they're simply an optical illusion. The slant of the hill makes it appear that the vehicles are coasting uphill when they are actually going down. Even a ball thrown down the hill appears to roll back up. The most famous is Magnetic Hill north of Moncton, New Brunswick, but there are also two in Ontario and two in Québec…perhaps there is even one in a town near you.

## Slam Dunk Impact Craters

Fortunately, we present-day humans have not yet had to experience one of the most dramatic events in geological history. We're talking an "end of the world" scenario, the Extinction Level Event (ELE) of Hollywood movies. It is none other than the dreaded "impact crater," the result of huge asteroids slamming into the Earth. It will happen again one day, but hopefully not too soon, because we know they have hit Canada at least 26 times in the past.

The biggest is the Sudbury Crater, which is 250 kilometres across and was caused when a huge hunk of space rock walloped right into the vicinity of the Giant Sudbury Nickel sculpture about 1.85 billion years before it was built. The Manicouagan impact crater, which smashed into Québec around 200 million years ago, formed today's Lake Manicouagan. When astronaut Marc Garneau saw it from space, he thought it looked like a giant eyeball staring back at him and called it the "Eye of Québec." One smaller earth impact crater is the Holleford meteor crater north of Kingston, measuring 2.35 kilometres in diameter. Discovered in 1955, it now appears more like a depression in the picturesque farmland, but when the 90-metre flaming rock came hurtling toward Earth some 550 million years ago, it probably outdid the best special effects Hollywood could ever muster.

# Mounds and Mounds

Technically, the grassy-covered mounds and earthworks found throughout many Canadian provinces are artificial, not natural. Yet the ones that have survived pioneer settlement, deforestation and mass urbanization often blend in so well with the landscape that many people don't even look twice at them. Mound building in North America dates back to 1000 BC. The builders, nomadic tribes from the mound-rich Ohio Valley, likely came up only during the warmer summer months. They created sites such as the Southwold Earthworks in Elgin County near Lake Erie.

A plaque at the Southwold Earthworks

Surrounded by farmland, these unusual earthworks were once a village occupied by the Attiwandaronk peoples, long before the Europeans arrived. Palisades built from tree trunks were placed in the ground and covered with earth, while temporary longhouses were built inside the compound. By 500 AD, the mound-building craze started to wane. Human construction methods took on a whole new meaning, and you won't believe what we built next....

# GETTING THERE

*One of the great things about Canada is that it's a big country with oodles of space, and we usually have more than enough raw materials to build whatever we like. Look at the great Canadian Pacific Railway or the world's longest highway—the Trans-Canada. You, too, can build whatever tickles your fancy. Make it as big as you like, as crazy as can be and as gaudy as possible. It can, and has, been done.*

## Like a Bridge Over Icy Waters

The superlative-long bridge theme continues with the "World's Longest Bridge Over Ice-covered Waters." Confederation Bridge opened in 1997 and at last connected Prince Edward Island to New Brunswick. Designed to withstand earthquakes as well as the wicked Maritime weather, the bridge contains high-wind buffer barriers and specially shaped pier bases meant to deflect ice floes. At 12.9 kilometres long, it has 17 closed-circuit television surveillance cameras and 34 traffic signals, which are thankfully almost always green because stopping on the bridge is not permitted (the traffic signals do control traffic if there is an accident or lane closure). You wouldn't want to stop and get out on this bridge anyway—the highest point is 60 metres above the water, and the strong winds would likely blow you into the Northumberland Strait. For this reason, pedestrians and bicycles are also not allowed on the bridge.

### Why the Bear Didn't Cross the Road

With millions of visitors per year, Banff National Park needed to find a solution to the age-old man versus nature debate when it came to roadways. How could the animals cross the heavily travelled Trans-Canada Highway without turning

the area into a watch-out-for-roadkill zone? The answer was 21 underpasses, a 2.4-metre-tall highway fence and two 50-metre-wide tree-covered overpasses built exclusively for the wildlife. During the first year after construction, only one black bear and a cougar used the $1 million overpasses. Eventually, elk, deer, moose and grizzly bears followed, while more black bears and cougars showed a preference for the underpasses. To date, wildlife collision rates are down by more than 80 percent. Best of all, no crossing guards were needed.

## Bridges to Somewhere

Hartland, New Brunswick, is home to the world's longest covered bridge. You can't miss it—it's the only one in town. Just look for the "World's Longest Covered Bridge" sign, the line-up of vehicles waiting to pass through (one at a time because there is no two-way traffic) and the understanding locals who wisely realize the monetary influx these summer tourist hordes bring. Covered bridges were once popular pioneer constructions in

Canadian provinces, but many fell into disrepair over the decades. In winter, snow was actually shovelled *into* the bridge so sleighs could glide through them more easily. The 339-metre-long Hartland bridge does have a romantic look about it. Legend has it that young couples would steal secret kisses as they passed through the darkened tunnel. Another tradition is to take a deep breath and make a wish before the bridge's entrance—if you can make to the other side without exhaling, your wish will be granted. At the height of tourist season, whether your wish comes true or you pass out first depends on how fast the line-up is moving.

## The Last Spike(s)

There were actually three "last spikes" driven in when the Canadian Pacific Railway was finally finished on November 7, 1885. A silver spike was made for the ceremony but wasn't used. A second iron spike turned into the "bent spike" when Lord Strathcona drove it into the railway crooked. He later took it out, shaved off parts of it and made them into diamond-encrusted jewellery pieces for his wife and other women. The last iron spike was the real deal, but CPR roadmaster Frank Brothers immediately dug it up since he didn't want souvenir hunters to ruin the track. The spike was presented to CPR President Edward Beatty, but nobody really knows where it is now.

## They Call This Union Station?

Toronto's downtown Union Station is perhaps the busiest train and commuter union station in Canada. But the smallest Union Station in North America can be found a few hours south, between the Ontario towns of Port Stanley and St. Thomas. This Union Station, a leftover from the railway days of the 19th century, was so small that CN forgot about it when they demolished many other unused railway stations. Not much bigger than the average living room, Union Station still proudly carries its place sign even though trains and passengers don't ever stop there.

### Secret Subway Station

Lower Bay Station, originally part of Toronto's subway system, was shut down in 1966 because the line involved trains reversing direction, which caused huge delays. The formerly abandoned station has since found new life as a subway workers' training venue and an often-used set for movies. For example, check out the 2006 thriller *16 Blocks* with Bruce Willis. Despite the fake New York City subway signage, it was actually filmed in Toronto's secret subway. (I worked there one night as a movie extra and stood within inches of Mr. *Die Hard* himself!)

# OTHER STRANGE STRUCTURES

## The Skinny on this Building

Chang Toy was the kind of guy who stood his ground, even if that ground was barely two metres wide. It all started in 1906 when Vancouver's city hall decided to widen Pender Street. In doing so, the city expropriated a seven-metre strip of land owned by the Sam Kee Company, a successful business run by Chang Toy and his partner, Shum Moon. Toy was left with a mere two-metre sliver of land, and the city refused to compensate Toy for his losses. In return, Toy staunchly refused to give it away or sell it cheaply. Instead, he hired an architect to design a building on the tiny strip of land, and in 1913, the structure became the world's narrowest commercial building. Chang died in 1920, but his thin building remains a famous landmark in Vancouver's Chinatown.

### Whiz Stations

When you gotta go, you gotta go, right? That may be, but if you're caught "spending a penny" in public, be prepared for a hefty ticket after you zip up your pants. It's an unpleasant problem, especially around big city entertainment districts where hundreds, even thousands, of partygoers congregate on weekend nights. All that drinking and lack of public facilities means those full-bladdered fellows (since the majority of culprits are drunken young men) will go anywhere from alleyways to planters. As one councillor put it, "The smell doesn't go away."

Most Canadian municipalities hand out fines that range anywhere from less than $100 to a stiff $500 ticket in Edmonton. The city of Victoria went one step further and launched an anti-public urination campaign, consisting of posters sporting slogans such as "Dude, Get A Handle On That Thing." Eventually, Victoria decided to try another solution—the "pissoirs," or public urinals. These plastic or stainless-steel devices made their mark in Europe a few years ago but have only recently come to Canadian soil, or rather Canadian concrete. After a few years of testing different portable devices, Victoria finally unveiled a new $40,000 public urinal on a downtown street in late 2009. With its curved, green, fence-like poles, the architecturally designed urinal has been described as a "piece of art." At one point, the city had considered the world's most state-of-the-art urinals from the Netherlands. Stored underground and activated to rise-up at night, the high-tech urinals would have been more aesthetically pleasing but purchasing problems nixed the expensive plan.

The city of Edmonton also announced that it will invest in keeping their "whiz stations" open 24/7 during the summer months. Each station has four urinals surrounded by a 1.2-metre-high "modesty fence." According to the director of the Old Strathcona Business Association, they "looked like giant washing machine agitators with narrow walls separating the spaces." Success was apparently measured in "liquid litres," and the city council now has a budget for both the portables and a permanent public facility. "We welcome all weak bladders," adds the director. Ah, what a relief!

## Bizarre Ice Hotel

If you like to sleep in a cold room, melt to the tunes of Vanilla Ice and enjoy "chilling out," then the Ice Hotel will be your ideal vacation hot spot. Just 25 minutes west of Québec City, this seasonal lodging is only open from early January to April because it's made entirely from 15,000 tonnes of snow and 500 tonnes of ice. The hotel design varies each year but usually consists of three dozen rooms, a chapel (130 couples have actually been married in the hotel since it opened in 1990), a cinema, an outdoor hot tub, an ice chandelier and the aptly named ice bar. Over half a million visitors have toured the Ice Hotel, and some 25,000 have actually

checked in. The four-foot-thick walls keep each room at an inside temperature between –2°C and –5°C. Guests sleep on ice beds piled high with furs and thermal sleeping bags. When spring arrives, the Ice Hotel has to be dismantled by machines since melting would take too long and leave one huge puddle.

## Cool Church

Where is the coolest place to worship in the far north? Inside an igloo-shaped church, of course. One such building is Our Lady of Victory on Inuvik's Mackenzie Road. With its silver dome, its white "snow-block-like" lines and its round, 23-metre diameter, this Roman Catholic church resembles a permanent igloo. The 2.5-metre cross on top gives its purpose away, but this creation was a labour of love. Designed by Brother Maurice Larocque, the church opened in 1960 after two years of construction. It cost only $70,000, and volunteers did almost all the work.

Building in the Arctic, however, was no easy task. Materials such as wood had to be transported some 1400 kilometres from the south.

There was also the problem of the permafrost, or frozen ground layer. Heat from the building could melt the permafrost and cause structural problems, so the church rests on a gravel-filled, saucer-shaped base.

Not to be outdone, Iqaluit built its own tourist landmark in 1970. St. Jude's Anglican Cathedral had a white half dome that also made it look like an igloo, but it was destroyed by arsonists in 2005. Parishioners still hope to raise enough money to build a new igloo of worship, perhaps one with the same "snow house" appeal but without all the snow.

 After a stop at the igloo church, tourists in Inuvik can warm up with a visit to the continent's most northerly greenhouse. The Inuvik Community Greenhouse was once an old arena, but it now grows bedding plants and hydroponic vegetables from May to September. Fresh arctic produce never tasted so good!

### The Long and Winding Road
The Wapusk Trail is the longest winter road in the world and likely the roughest. It can take anywhere from 12 to 15 hours to make the 752-kilometre trip between Peananuck, Ontario, and Gillam, Manitoba. *Wapusk* means "white bear" in Cree, and this seasonal road is certainly prone to whiteout conditions. Most of the road is built over frozen muskeg, and during snowstorms, search-and-rescue crews are often called in to help people stuck in snowdrifts.

## Screaming Tunnel
Just past St. Catharines, Ontario, on the way to Niagara Falls is a dead-end rural road with an old drainage tunnel on one side. "Dead" is the key word because legend has it a young girl perished there during the late 19th century. Her clothes caught

on fire, and she ran through the tunnel screaming. Apparently, if you light a match in the tunnel, her spirit will blow it out, and you may even hear her screams. Then again, it may just be a bunch of drunken teenagers shrieking or an actor rehearsing. The "Screaming Tunnel" was also used as the set for a murder scene in David Cronenberg's horror flick, *The Dead Zone*, based on Stephen King's novel of the same name.

## Yorkville Rock

Unless they're part of a landscaping company, most giant rocks are only moved by glaciers—but not the Yorkville Rock. All 650 tonnes of this billion-year-old rock was transported from Gravenhurst, Ontario, to downtown Toronto by truck. In 1991, the city of Toronto wanted to build a nice park on an unattractive block in the heart of Yorkville Village, and architect Olesand

Worland was hired to design something to represent the ecology of the province. Since Ontario has a diverse environment, Worland took the "a bit of this and a bit of that" approach. He placed trees at one end to represent Ontario's forests, a pond to symbolize the wetlands and an herb garden to embody its agriculture. When it came to a representation of the Canadian Shield, Worland went straight to the source. A chunk of rock was cut out at Gravenhurst, hacked into more manageable pieces and re-assembled when it arrived in Toronto. After a cost of $300,000, the park opened in 1994. It's a little bit of country amid the high-end Yorkville boutiques, all thanks to a rock that was rolled in on a flat-bed truck.

In July 2001, volunteer firefighters in Elm Creek, Manitoba, built a large fire hydrant that measured over nine metres high. Which makes one wonder...either they didn't have enough fires to keep them busy, or they had so many that they needed a *really* big fire hydrant.

## Ugly Faces at Old City Hall

Toronto's Old City Hall on Bay Street is a perfect example of
the Victorian Romanesque Revival architectural style. Its ornate
design features more than a few gargoyle-like creatures reminiscent of those found on medieval European cathedrals—but look
closely over the entrance archways and you'll see some very
unattractive human faces. Could these unsightly visages actually
be...city councillors? When architect E.J. Lennox was building
the City Hall, he had some negative run-ins with the politicians.
The structure was finally completed in 1899, but not before
Lennox got a little payback. Apparently, he fashioned the faces
after the city councillors but with grotesque, distorted expressions.
Lennox put his own face on one of the archways as well—his
is the one with the pleasant appearance and the fashionable
handlebar moustache.

# The Mall

Most shopping malls aren't very bizarre—there are the usual stores,
the food courts and the fake Santa at Christmastime. When
you've got the largest indoor shopping mall in the world, however,
that's totally jaw-dropping. West Edmonton Mall in Alberta is
absolutely huge. It's like an indoor shopping mall that goes on
forever, which isn't a bad thing when you consider that Edmonton
is prone to some of the coldest winters around, and nobody

wants to shop outside in that kind of weather. We're talking over 800 stores, 26 movie theatres and more than 110 restaurants. It boasts the world's largest indoor amusement park, the world's largest indoor triple-loop roller coaster, the world's largest indoor lake, the world's largest indoor permanent wave pool and, of course, the world's largest car-park. And if you lose your vehicle in one of the 20,000 parking spots, well, that can lead to the world's largest headache.

## Do the Time...If You Can Fit In

There's stiff competition as to which town lays claim to the title of North America's smallest jail. Built in 1890, the two-cell structure in Rodney, near London, Ontario, measures a mere 24.3 square metres, or 4.5 metres by 5.4 metres, and still bears its original steel-bar cell doors. Any prisoners held there now will have only tourist brochures to read because it also doubles as a visitor information centre during the summer. Port Dalhousie near St. Catharines, Ontario, had a tiny jail as well, but it's now part of a bar. Tweed, in central-eastern Ontario, claimed that its small jail—now a community policing station—was only 4.9 metres by 6.1 metres. Other Ontario towns with mini-jails include Creemore, Providence Bay and Coboconk, as well as Barens River, a former gold mining town north of Red Lake.

# A DIFFERENT KIND OF BUILDER

## Ontario's Taj Mahal

If there were an award for the Most Romantic Canadian, Thomas Foster may just win hands-down—anyone who builds a mini Taj Mahal for his deceased wife surely makes the cut. Born in Toronto in 1852, Foster worked as a butcher and businessman before making his fortune in real estate. He married Elizabeth McCauley in 1893 and later went into politics. The Fosters had only one daughter, Ruby, but she died at the tender age of 10 in 1904. After his wife's death 16 years later, Foster became something of a workaholic. Known as "Honest Tom," he served as mayor of Toronto from 1925 to 1927, but when he wasn't re-elected, Foster decided to go out and travel the world.

It was during a visit to India's Taj Mahal—the magnificent memorial built in the 17th century by Shah Jahan as a final resting place for his own beloved wife—that Foster became inspired. When he returned to Canada, he commissioned architects J.H. Craig and H.H. Madill to design a Taj Mahal–type mausoleum right on his property in rural Uxbridge. Finished in 1935, the $250,000 building is made of limestone and marble with a copper dome and 12 stained glass windows. Inside is a marble altar and pulpit with terrazzo floors, marble mosaics as well as three crypts for his wife, his daughter and himself. Foster was finally able to rest in his masterpiece for eternity when he died in 1945 at the age of 93.

### The Old Walt Rock

Then again, if you admire someone, why not carve their name into a rock? Flora MacDonald Denison was a big fan of the American poet, Walt Whitman. She appreciated his "democratic ideals" so much that she had lines from one of Whitman's poems engraved onto the 100-metre-high granite rock on Mazinaw Lake to create a giant dedication to her hero. Visitors to the rock, now part of Bon Echo Provincial Park in Ontario, can still see the foot-high letters that were chiselled in the summer of 1919. Rumour has it that tourists may even catch a glimpse of the ghost of Old Walt himself.

## Stonewall

If you've got a few decades to spare, why not build a wall of stone? That's precisely what Albert Johnson did on his property just outside Kindersley, Saskatchewan. He started in 1962 and took about 40 years to complete the structure, one stone at a time. Made without cement or mortar, the stone wall is about one kilometre long and two metres high. It may not be as impressive as another famous wall in China, but this is definitely the one and only Great Wall of Saskatchewan.

# That's ONE CRAZY CANUCK!

## Bill Lishman: Architect, Sculptor and Goose Imprinter Extraordinaire

Bill Lishman liked to build, and do, some unusual things—very unusual things. During his school years, Lishman struggled with dyslexia and colour blindness. He did have a knack for art and obtained high marks in sculpture during his one and only year at the Ontario College of Art. In the late 1960s, Lishman picked up $6 worth of scrap metal and welded together a large, steel Trojan-like horse statue. Late one night, he and a friend secretly placed it right smack in front of Toronto City Hall. It was a great publicity stunt, but Lishman was just getting warmed up. Inspired by the 1969 moon landing, Lishman decided to make and film a replica lunar module he called "Moonship on Earth." After completing the project, Lishman strung it with lights and placed it out on the road near his home. Thinking it was a recently landed spacecraft, passersby stopped and stared.

Lishman had always had an interest in flight, especially flying with birds. He even raised Canadian geese by hand and successfully taught them to fly behind a boat and later an ultralight plane. After they hatched, the goslings were "imprinted" by Lishman and his children, who carried around tape recorders playing ultralight motor sounds. Lishman's work with imprinting and geese migration later became the basis of the 1996 Hollywood movie, *Fly Away Home*, starring Jeff Bridges and Anna Paquin.

Lishman and his wife, Paula, a textile artist, even designed a unique home for themselves near Lake Scugog, Ontario.

Built partially underground in a hill, the dome shape of the house has a grass-covered roof and skylights to let in natural light.

One of Lishman's best-known works of art was Autohenge, which is exactly what it sounds like. When Chrysler contracted Lishman to make a promotional sculpture for its Plymouth Sundance and Dodge Shadow in 1986, Lishman went to a field north of Oshawa and erected a replica of the famous English Stonehenge. This one, however, was made entirely of cars, most of which were perched on their bumpers like metal monoliths The Autohenge sculpture was widely photographed, and even though Lishman later created an Icehenge on Lake Scugog, it didn't achieve the same international success as Autohenge. If it hadn't been taken down in the early 1990s, perhaps Autohenge would still be standing today, just like its Druidic inspiration thousands of kilometres away.

## Cosmic Calendar

No need to travel to Great Britain to visit Stonehenge—there may be one right here in Canada. Gordon Freeman, a retired university professor, has spent the last three decades studying a 26-square-kilometre site east of Calgary near Brooks. In his book, *Canada's Stonehenge*, Freeman describes the tell-tale patterns in the placement of the large rocks throughout the area and concludes they must be part of an ancient, 5000-year-old

Britain's Stonehenge

astronomical temple. If true, it would predate Britain's Stonehenge and even the Egyptian pyramids. While some archaeologists claim the rocks were randomly distributed by glaciers, Freeman believes their alignments are uncannily precise. His thousands of photographs show how they accurately mark the spring and fall equinoxes and constellations just like other solar and lunar calendars.

## The Unsinkable Ship

There's a full-sized ship in the middle of the Canadian Prairies. This unlikely find sits on a concrete base at a pioneer village south of Moose Jaw and is the work of the late Tom Sukanen, a Finnish shipbuilder. Sukanen arrived in Minnesota as an immigrant, but in 1911, he left his wife and children and moved to a farm in Saskatchewan. After seven years, he returned for his family but found out his wife had since died and his children had been taken into foster care. He ended up walking the 1000 kilometres back to Saskatchewan with grand plans to build a ship and sail home to Finland. Sukanen poured all his time and money into the *Sontiainen*, the Finnish word for "little dung beetle." In 1941, the ship was vandalized, and Sukanen was committed to an institution where he died a couple of years later. The ship languished until 1972, when a Moose Jaw farmer took it upon himself to restore the ship. Once completed, Tom Sukanen's remains were exhumed and reburied next to his beloved *Sontiainen*.

# BIZARRE BOTTLE BUILDINGS

## The Embalming Fluid Bottle House

Bizarre can also be beautiful when it glistens in the sun like a precious gemstone. Such is a unique house near Boswell, British Columbia. Look closely and you'll see that its elegant construction material is none other than glass bottles, and not just any bottles. This house was made entirely with embalming fluid bottles. That's right, embalming fluid—the same stuff that is piped through the veins of cadavers in a funeral home. But who would collect over half a million empty, 455-millilitre embalming fluid bottles and have the time to build an entire house with them? A retired undertaker, of course.

His name was David Brown, a veteran funeral director who later worked part time selling embalming fluid to funeral homes. In the days before recycling, Brown's customers were more than happy to give him their empties. When Brown retired in 1952, he began to construct his dream home on an idyllic outcropping overlooking Kootenay Lake. For two years, he polished and cemented each rectangular bottle into place, with the bottoms facing out. The walls were one bottle thick, complete with wiring around the bottlenecks, and finished with cedar boards on the inside. Thankfully, Brown had the foresight to construct the house on a solid granite footing since its final weight was some 455 tonnes. It was also well insulated because the air inside the bottles provided the equivalent of 70 centimetres of fibreglass batting. Brown and his wife soon moved out of their nearby temporary trailer and into their new castle-like home, complete with archways and turrets. Word of the intriguing residence spread, and soon Brown had to hire tour guides to satisfy his many visitors. He died in 1970, but the Bottle House still attracts tourists from around the world.

## The Beer Bottle Wall

The same year David Brown began his bottle house was coincidentally the same year Geordie Dobson arrived in Keno City, Yukon. Once a bustling silver mining town during the '20s and '30s, Keno City was left with barely 100 residents some 20 years later. Geordie, who was originally from Scotland, loved the place because he said he could "do whatever I want. I could shoot a moose when I want..." He could also collect all the empty beer bottles he wanted. By the late 1960s, he had over 32,000 and took the next four years to cement them to the exterior of his house. "They make the best insulation you can get," Geordie said. I'm not sure if Geordie has heard of David Brown, but I'm sure he'd agree that great minds think alike.

### The PEI Bottle Houses
In 1979, Edouard Arsenault of Cap-Egmont, PEI, received a postcard from his daughter describing BC's famous Bottle House. The next year, Edouard started his own creation from

a pile of bottles he had collected over the winter. He used over 25,000 bottles to make three buildings, including a six-gabled house, a tavern and a chapel. Although harsh winters later damaged the buildings, they were restored in the 1990s and have remained a popular tourist destination ever since. Which makes one think, if every visitor was invited to BYOB, wouldn't they have enough to build even more bottle houses?

## Bob's Bottle House

The bottle house idea was definitely popular in 1979. That was also the year Bob Cain and his wife Dora started collecting the 4000 glass bottles it took to make their own one-room bottle house north of Treherne, Manitoba. In 1983, they collected another 5000 bottles and built a small church, complete with stained glass windows. They also built a wishing well with 500 bottles and used another 1000 to create an outdoor bathroom for visitors.

# BUILDING BIG THINGS

## Making the Big Time

Sometimes, you simply need to create a huge, enormous, extraordinary...well, whatever you call it, it's big:

*Cut Knife, Saskatchewan:* What else but a 16-metre-high tomahawk?

*Davidson, Saskatchewan:* A leaning coffee pot, naturally tilted toward an equally gigantic mug.

*Kimberley, BC:* The largest working cuckoo clock in North America commemorates the "Bavarian City of the Rockies."

*Maugerville, New Brunswick:* A huge, smiling, waving potato greets customers at Harvey's roadside vegetable market.

*Moonbeam, Ontario:* A 5.5-metre-wide flying saucer, what else?

*Plaster Rock, New Brunswick:* A giant fiddlehead sculpture stands in honour of the area's tasty fiddleheads.

*Rocanville, Saskatchewan:* A giant squirting oil can to commemorate the oil can capital of the world.

*Sparwood, BC:* Terex Titan is the world's biggest dump truck and was brought to the coal mines in 1978. Retired in 1990, the 20-metre-long truck has 10 enormous, 3.3-metre-wide tires (that's 11 feet across, each!), once held 3600 litres of fuel and now sits outside a visitor information centre.

*St. Claude, Manitoba:* A six-metre-long smoking pipe, in remembrance of the settlers from the pipe-making town of Jura, France.


## Giant People

*Canora, Saskatchewan:* "Leslie" is a 7.6-metre-high Ukrainian woman dressed in Ukrainian clothes with a traditional welcoming tray of bread and salt.

*Flin Flon, Manitoba:* "Flinty," a seven-metre-tall statue, also known as Professor Josiah Flintabbatey Flonatin, is a science-fiction character and the city's namesake.

*Fort St. John, BC:* "Muffler Man" is a muscular big guy with a construction hat, plaid shirt and carrying an axe.

*Taber, Alberta:* "Kirk's Tire Lady," an attractive brunette originally from Lethbridge, was moved almost 50 kilometres east to Taber. She stands in front of the store in her short blue skirt and red top, with one arm raised as if to say "Come on over!"

# ODD ANCIENT ONES

*We tend to imagine Canada as a kind of vast hunting preserve convenient to the United States.*

–Edmund Wilson, famed American writer and social critic

*The animal kingdom has always been fascinating, and Canadian creatures are no exception. This land is home to some very distinctive living things and a few giant fibreglass ones, too.*

## Glad He's Extinct?

The world's biggest trilobite was found near Churchill, Manitoba, in 1998. For those who don't know what a trilobite is, just imagine a joint-legged creature that's a distant relative of a crab or scorpion and that roamed around the bottom of the seas during the Paleozoic Era, about 445 million years ago when Canada was more tropical in climate (I know, hard to imagine). Most fossilized trilobites measure less than 10 centimetres long, but the one now located in Winnipeg's Manitoba Museum is a whopping 72 centimetres in length. That's one mega-crabby bottom-feeder, indeed!

### Tiniest Dinosaur Footprints

Little birdlike footprints must be from a bird, right? In 1984, a fossil collector spied the world's smallest dinosaur footprints near Parrsboro, Nova Scotia. The dino tracks are displayed in the Parrsboro Rock and Mineral Shop and Museum. Chalk one up for the theory that birds evolved from dinosaurs.

## Giant Dino Turd

Saskatchewan is home to the world's largest carnivore coprolite ever found—yes, that's fossilized feces—a huge dino turd left behind by Scotty the Tyrannosaurus Rex. Found in 1995 near Swift Current, this whitish-grey, big piece of, well, you know what, measures half a metre across and weighs seven kilograms.

# ANIMAL TALES

## Watch Your Garbage...and Your Pet!

It's a jungle out in the urban ecosystem of Toronto. Coyotes, those mangy wild dogs, are usually shy but have been known to venture into cities in search of dinner, which could be either mice, rabbits, cats or small dogs. One coyote even snatched a pet Chihuahua from a private backyard in Toronto's trendy Beaches neighbourhood. With ravines and treed areas in close proximity, it's also a perfect place for raccoons to raise their families. But when they're hungry, these masked bandits will raid your garbage like it's an all-you-can-eat buffet. Toronto is the raccoon capital of North America—and likely the world—with close to 100 raccoons per square kilometre. Rural areas usually have only 4 to 12 *Procyon lotor* (the scientific term for raccoon) per square kilometre.

### Snake and Salamanders

Ophidiophobes beware—you may wish to avoid Narcisse, Manitoba, during snake mating season. Manitoba has the world's largest population of red-sided garter snakes, and the creviced limestone rock of the area makes it a snake den heaven. More than 70,000 snakes hibernate there over the winter but slither out come spring. With increased traffic, and therefore more snake pancakes, conservationists even constructed little tunnels under the main highway in 2000 so the snakes could safely migrate across. At the Narcisse Snake Dens, tourists can view more snakes from special viewing platforms. It may be a bit voyeuristic; when they tangle together in a giant snake ball, they're actually mating, but if you didn't freak out during the snake scene in *Indiana Jones and the Raiders of the Lost Ark*, then this is the place to be.

If you want to see salamanders, check out Saltcoats, just south of Yorkton, Saskatchewan, the tiger salamander hub of Canada. On rainy days, you'll see thousands of slippery salamanders dodge vehicles as they dash toward the nearby Anderson Lake.

## Return of the Swans

The tundra swans are coming! The tundra swans are coming! It's a sea of white at the Old Thedford Bog near Grand Bend, Ontario, during late March. Upwards of 10,000 tundra swans gather in the area for a rest stop on their annual 3000-kilometre migration from the east Atlantic coast to their breeding grounds in the Arctic. Formerly known as the whistling swan, the tundra swan makes a distinct sound, likely the feathered equivalent of "are we there yet?"

## Name That Animal

When the first horse arrived in New France in 1663, the First Nation peoples were so intrigued by its appearance that they called it the Frenchman's moose. As for the caribou, its name actually means "snow shoveller" in the Mi'kmaq language, which makes perfect sense because these animals do push away, or "shovel," the snow with their antlers to get at the food underneath it. The word "chipmunk," however, is *atchitamon* in Ojibwa, which means "head first," as in the way these critters go down trees. Perhaps it should translate as "indecisive rodent who gets squished when he crosses road." And in 2006, an American hunter shot a grizzly-polar bear hybrid animal in the Northwest Territories. A similarly strange, cross-breed bear was killed by an

Inuit hunter in April 2010. The animal had the coat of a polar bear but patches of brown hair and a large head identical to a grizzly's. Was it a grolar bear or a pizzly? The jury is still out.

## Don't Poke the Bear

Warning: do not wear a polar bear costume on Halloween in Churchill, Manitoba. Locals might think you're the real thing and try to tranquilize you on sight. There's a reason why Churchill is known as the "Polar Bear Capital." Every October, 100 or so of the giant white beasts wander through town on their migration route toward Hudson Bay (technically, polar bears don't have white hair—it's colourless and simply appears white, but if you're close enough to tell the difference, then you've got bigger problems, such as the fact that the average polar bear's paw is larger than your face). The day before Halloween, local police, park wardens and firefighters keep an eye out for any stray bears so kids are safe to trick-or-treat on October 31. Churchill even has a polar bear jail, a type of holding tank where the mammals are held until they can be safely transported back to the ice floes.

The Northwest Territories and Nunavut have the distinction of being the only regions in the world with polar bear–shaped licence plates. Now that's better than forking out the dough for a vanity plate, don't you think?

# RASCALLY RODENTS

*The beaver, which has come to represent Canada as the eagle does the United States and the lion Britain, is a flat-tailed, slow-witted, toothy rodent known to bite off its own testicles or to stand under its own falling trees.*

–June Callwood, Canadian journalist, author and social activist

## All Hail the Beaver

When rumours swirled in the mid-1970s that New York was about to proclaim the beaver as their official state animal, Canadian politicians took a rare, unified stance. They passed a bill in 1975 to "provide recognition of the beaver as a symbol of the sovereignty of Canada." How could it not be? The buck-toothed beaver has been a Canadian icon for hundreds of years. The beaver also has one very attractive, and very valuable, feature—a dense, silky and super-soft underfur. Beaver fur is the main reason this country became what it is today. Thanks to this chunky rodent and the rabid fur trade it engendered, we're a civilized (ahem) society. Unfortunately, the fur trade almost hunted the beaver to extinction by the early 20th century until regulations were put in place to ensure the beavers' numbers increased.

## Damn Dams

The beaver has graced our five-cent coin and historic stamps, and more than a few people suggested Toronto's "Skydome" (now the Rogers Centre) be called "The Beaver Dome" when it was built in 1987. But, while we may think beavers are harmless, cute and cuddly, their dams have been known to leave humans cursing "those damn beavers." On May 8, 1984, a CPR train hit a beaver dam, burst a tank and derailed near Chalk River, causing $1.5 million damage.

# Black, Red and White

Cute, black squirrels are common in Ontario and Québec, but the farther south you travel, the harder they are to find. Interestingly, Exeter, Ontario, is one of those rare places with a noticeable population of white "albino" squirrels. It all depends on where you are, because in Montréal most squirrels are grey while in Toronto they're mostly black. You might even spy a reddish one or (and I've seen this) a black one with a red tail. The surprising fact is that black, red or white, technically these squirrels all belong to the species, *Sciurus carolinensis*, also known as the eastern grey squirrel. Go figure.

In 2004, four squirrels that had become knotted together at the tails were taken to a veterinarian's office in Weyburn, Saskatchewan. "It moved kind of like an octopus," said the veterinarian as he described the twisted, frightened clump of rodents. The squirrels were temporarily anesthetized and their tails quickly untangled.

## Refugee Rodent

Sometimes, the government can be a hard nut to crack. An immigration situation went squirrelly after Sabrina, the flying squirrel, was ordered deported to the U.S. a mere three months after her arrival in Canada. Steve Patterson, a naturalist and school teacher, went to Indiana to buy the young squirrel. He filled out the required forms and declared her to customs at the border without a hitch. Sabrina settled nicely into her new home, or rather her nest box, at Patterson's residence in Mississauga. She ate fruit, bonded with her owner and was even potty-trained to go on a plastic tray. Patterson continued to raise Sabrina as a "working squirrel," the star in presentations he gave to school children.

Then federal officials contacted him with the news that they had made a mistake. Apparently, an outbreak of the monkey pox virus meant that any U.S. rodents were no longer allowed to be imported into Canada. Even though Sabrina was healthy, the Canadian Food Inspection Agency said she would have to leave. Patterson refused to hand her over, and that's when the fur really began to fly. The case went to federal court in October 2004, but with the public's support and help from a few high-profile lawyers, the government finally gave in. The Health of Animal's Act was changed to allow squirrels and other rodents like Sabrina to stay "for educational purposes."

# They Call It a "Donovan Bailey"

The fastest land animal in North America was almost extinct at the beginning of the 20th century but has made a strong comeback. The fleet-footed pronghorn, which can run up to 86 kilometres per hour, zips around the fields of southwestern Alberta and southeastern Saskatchewan and never worries about getting a speeding ticket.

## Gopher Museum

The rural town of Torrington, Alberta, has a giant 3.7-metre-tall gopher statue and the world's only Gopher Museum. In it, you'll find dozens of stuffed gophers posed and dressed in costumes. Among others, there's a gopher priest, a gopher clown, a gopher

firefighter, a gopher beautician and gopher Olympic medalists (what sport gophers compete in, I have no idea). The museum, however, has generated a "hole" lot of controversy from animal rights groups, mainly because the gophers had to be hunted and killed to participate in the exhibit. Townsfolk replied "get stuffed" and pointed out the damage these gophers caused to crops and fields. Ironically, the media publicity attracted thousands more tourists to the museum since it opened in 1996.

# FAR OUT FELINES

## The Cat Came Back

Hamlet the cat escaped from his cage in the cargo hold of a plane taking off from Toronto and eluded capture for almost seven weeks. When he was finally found in February 1984, Hamlet had travelled well over 600,000 kilometres.

### Parliamentary Kitties

Sometime in the 1970s, animal lover Irène Desormeaux decided to take a little food to the feral cats behind Parliament Hill in Ottawa. The cats appreciated the gesture and stuck around. Rumour has it the cats were always welcome in the Parliament buildings because they chased the rodents away. Although that may or may not be true (and while some might argue that the federal government is infested with rats), a couple dozen stray cats, all now appropriately spayed and neutered, still make the area their home. What's more, they live in their very own wooden shelter, a type of miniature Parliament Hill cat house, built by their elderly volunteer caretaker.

Jake, an orange tabby born in Bonfield, Ontario, in 2002, holds a world record for the cat born with the most toes. The polydactyl feline boasts a total of 28 toes, seven on each paw, while normal cats only have 18 toes in total.

## Don't Hate Me Because I'm Beautiful

There's nothing more adorable than a cute, furry kitten—or, for that matter, a hairless one. The Sphynx breed of cat, also known as the Canadian Hairless, originated when a bald kitten was born to a Toronto breeder in 1966. Now, the Sphynx is one of the more rare and valuable breeds around, easily fetching over $1000 each.

The naked pussycats even hit the silver screen when a Sphynx actor-cat named Ted Nude-Gent portrayed Dr. Evil's pet cat, Mr. Bigglesworth, in Canadian Mike Myer's *Austin Powers* comedies. According to the plot, Mr. Bigglesworth used to be a fluffy long-haired cat until time-travel rendered him hairless. Dr. Evil's diminutive clone, Mini-Me, also has a similar cat, played by another Sphynx, Paul Nudeman. The part was originally given to Mel Gibskin, but he grew out of kittenhood too fast for filming.

# CELEBRITY ANIMALS

## Muddy the Mudcat

Situated along the Grand River, not far from Hamilton, Ontario, is the small town of Dunnville. If you like grabbing a beer, heading down to the river and fishing, then Dunnville is *the* place to be. The Grand River is full of these homely channel catfish, or "mudcats" as they're commonly called. When Dunnville residents received a "beautification" grant from the county, they decided to build a giant 15-metre-long metal mudcat. "Muddy" was officially unveiled on November 14, 2009, with hopes that the huge catch will be a big draw for the catfish-loving town of Dunnville.

### Extra-large Lobster

The town of Shediac, Nova Scotia, likes to call itself the "Lobster Capital of the World." Sure, the place draws thousands to its annual Lobster Festival and, yes, we all know it is home to a giant, 11-metre-high iron-and-concrete lobster sculpture. But the real mega-crustacean was caught in the Bay of Fundy in July 2008. Big Dee-Dee, a massive 10-kilogram lobster, made a splash after it ended up in a tank at Shediac's Big Fish seafood store. When

an auction for the decades old lobster was announced, half the bidders wanted to release it back into the ocean, while the other half hoped to enjoy Big Dee-Dee with melted butter. Despite bids reaching almost $5000, Big Dee-Dee's tail was saved when the owner decided to donate it to the Huntsman Marine Science Centre in St. Andrews, New Brunswick.

In 2009, Fiona, a rare yellow lobster, was caught off the coast of PEI and sent with the daily catch to Cape Cod, Massachusetts. There, a restaurant owner recognized her exceptional colouring and contacted the media. When the Huntsman Marine Science Centre heard about the lobster, they offered her a place at their aquarium. The Centre has since become a lobster haven with its latest addition, a bright-blue lobster from Maine named Lily.

## The Wiarton Willie Scandal

The town of Wiarton, Ontario, takes their albino groundhog mascot, Willie, very seriously. In 1995, they unveiled a giant statue, "Willie Emerging," on the lakeside overlooking Georgian Bay in homage to him. Wiarton Willie is part of an elite club of furry North American forecasters that make an appearance every February 2, on Groundhog Day. If the groundhog sees his shadow, there will be six more weeks of winter. On the other hand, if he doesn't, get ready for an early spring. The roots of this strange festival derive from Candlemas, the Christian festival of lights at the midpoint of winter. In German tradition, it's a badger that looks for his shadow, not a rodent. Pennsylvanian settlers introduced Punxsutawney Phil as their rodent prognosticator in 1886, and Canadian versions include Schubenacadie Sam in Nova Scotia and Alberta's Balzac Billy, though Wiarton Willie is perhaps Canada's best-known animal diviner.

Large crowds and throngs of media double the town's population on Willie's big day, and the annual Groundhog Festival pumps about $750,000 into the local economy. It all began in 1956, when a local resident, Mac McKenzie, jokingly sent out invitations for the first International Groundhog Day celebration. One duped reporter actually arrived to cover the "event" and found McKenzie drinking in a bar with friends. Not wanting to go home without a story, the reporter asked for a photo, so McKenzie stuck a white, furry hat in the snow and said that was the "groundhog." The next year, a small but genuine festival began, and eventually, Wiarton Willie took centre stage. All went well with subsequent Groundhog Days until late January 1999, when the 22-year-old Willie was found dead. Unable to locate a quick substitute, the announcement of Willie's untimely demise was made that February 2 in front of the anticipatory crowds. Out came a tiny, open coffin containing Willie, holding a bright-orange carrot between his paws. Schoolchildren bawled their eyes out and sympathies poured in from around the world. After the wake, rumours swirled that the body in the coffin was actually a stuffed imposter and that the real Willie's remains had been too badly decomposed for display. The shocking news made headlines, but eventually, three new male albino groundhogs were found to replace Willie. The trio even moved into a fancy $20,000 home, the Willie House, a three-metre-by-four-metre concrete-encased pen apparently designed with input from the Toronto Zoo.

Yet scandal rocked the town once again in 2003 when local residents grew concerned that two of the three "Willies" had not been seen for months. The absent groundhogs were eventually discovered dead in a three-metre-long tunnel, which was not part of the original Willie House design but was connected to an out-door cage play area. Town councillors demanded an explanation from the groundhogs' handler as to why they had learned of the missing animals from a member of the public. Many were upset that the surviving Willie had spent eight months alone with two dead bodies. Although the cause of death was thought to be drowning or hypothermia, there is another possibility. Male groundhogs are highly territorial and aggressive with each other. They also emerge from hibernation not because it's warm outside, but to mate. Could there have been a violent domestic war in the Willie House? Who knows, but don't be surprised if crowds come to see a Wiarton Wilhemina one Groundhog Day.

## Fred the Frog

Local historical museums are traditionally quaint venues full of artifacts, sketches, antique displays and mannequins dressed in pioneer clothing. These informative kiosks can be found in hundreds of towns across Canada, often housed in old heritage buildings or tourist offices as an ode to a rich cultural past.

In the York-Sunbury Historical Society Museum in Fredericton, New Brunswick, you can find one well-preserved, stuffed specimen—a 19-kilogram frog. At least, we think he was once alive. In 1885, a frog jumped into Fred Coleman's boat. Fred decided to take the amphibian home and gave it as much food as it wished until it ballooned to its present size—but that's just one story. Another is that Fred (the frog) lived in a nearby lake but was killed when a few unscrupulous men threw dynamite in to get some fish the easy way. Finally, there is the possibility Fred was not actually a real frog but a fake prop once used in a drug store to sell a "frog-in-your-throat" cough medicine. Perhaps, but that's highly unlikely, right?

# Colossal Creatures

Here's a collection of Canadian "Big" Animals, guaranteed not to eat or stomp on you:

*Boissevain, Manitoba:* "Tommy," a 6.7-metre-tall, flag-waving turtle on its rear legs, built in 1974 for the now-defunct turtle races derby.

*Falher, Alberta:* As the "Honeybee Capital of Canada," Falher boasts a seven-metre-long honeybee.

*Glenboro, Manitoba:* "Sara," a five-metre-high camel that guards Glenboro and looks north toward the Manitoba Desert (also known as the Spirit Sands sandhills in a nearby provincial park).

*Kyle, Saskatchewan:* "Wally," a 3.6-metre-tall woolly mammoth, in honour of a real one found nearby in 1964.

*La Rivière, Manitoba:* A nearly three-metre-high wild turkey made in 1986.

*Macklin, Saskatchewan:* A giant horse's ankle, seeing as the town hosts the World Bunnock Championships (bunnock is an old Russian game of tossing horse ankle bones).

*Moose Jaw, Saskatchewan:* "Mac the Moose," a 10-metre-tall, metal-and-cement sculpture created in 1984 to draw tourists to this southern Saskatchewan town.

*New Liskeard, Ontario:* "Ms. Claybelt," a giant fibreglass Holstein cow parked right near a McDonald's.

*Porcupine Plain, Saskatchewan:* At almost four metres in height, "Quilly Willy" is the world's largest porcupine.

*Turtleford, Saskatchewan:* "Big Ernie," an 8.5-metre-long turtle, but, unlike Boissevain's turtle, Ernie stands on all fours.

*Tisdale, Saskatchewan:* Look for the giant five-metre-long honeybee; along with rapeseed, it's part of the town's motto—"The Land of Rape and Honey."


## Jumbo Derailed

Poor Jumbo the Elephant—he probably wanted nothing more in life than to roam happily in his African homeland, but it was not meant to be. Instead, he was taken to France in 1863 and, two years later, settled into the London Zoo. As the first African elephant in England, Jumbo became quite a celebrity. When he was sold to the Barnum and Bailey Circus in 1882, Jumbo didn't want to leave and reportedly sat down in the middle of the street, refusing to budge. Somehow, Jumbo ended up on a ship to America and began his new career. He travelled by rail with the famous circus in a specially built carriage and was accompanied by another smaller elephant, Tom Thumb.

Back in the late 19th century, the southwestern Ontario town of St. Thomas, near London, was quite the railway hub. Townsfolk were thrilled when the circus stopped in, but tragedy struck shortly after a performance on September 15, 1885. As Jumbo and Tom Thumb were being led to their railway car, another train suddenly approached and caused a massive derailment. One of Jumbo's tusks tore through his brain, while Tom Thumb suffered a broken leg. Scott, the elephants' keeper, was unharmed but could do nothing for his beloved Jumbo as the great elephant passed away. Jumbo was gone, but not entirely. His hide was mounted as a circus attraction for a while before being donated to a Boston museum. A museum fire in 1975 destroyed the elephant skin, but Jumbo's skeleton can still be seen today at the New York Museum of Natural History.

Here in Canada, Jumbo is immortalized by a life-sized statue erected in 1985 to commemorate the 100th anniversary of his death. He stands, his trunk raised in salute to all who pass through St. Thomas. At least he'll be remembered forever.

# ARE THEY REAL?

## Huge, Hairy and Bizarre

In March 2007, Conservative MP Mike Lake brought forward a petition to grant the Sasquatch (called Bigfoot in the U.S.) status as an endangered species. Although Lake admitted that he didn't think the Sasquatch was real, and the petition never did make it much further, there have been hundreds of documented sightings of a giant, furry, upright creature roaming western Canada. Native accounts speak of a three-metre-tall creature, and another account from 1811 wrote of "the track of a large animal...the ball of the foot sunk three inches lower than the toes, the hinder part of the foot did not mark well; the length fourteen inches by eight inches in breadth...we were in no hurry to follow him." Were these the first records of Sasquatch footprints? Tracks found near the Skeena River in 1977 were 43 centimetres long. Some cryptozoologists think Sasquatch could be a lost species related to the ancient ape, "Gigantopithecus."

# Newsflash: Punk Beasts Terrify Girls

In 1913, two young girls saw a pair of giant ape-like beasts in Traverspine, near Goose Bay, Labrador. The creatures were uprooting rotten logs, as if looking for food; the larger of the two was over two metres tall, with long arms and white hair on top of his head. The girls' screams alerted their mother, who reached for a shotgun. She caught a glimpse of the white-haired beast and fired into the bushes. The mother later discovered blood on the ground and 30-centimetre-long tracks. Having previously killed 12 bears, the mother was adamant that these creatures were not bears.

### Wacko Jacko?

In July 4, 1884, the *Victoria Times Colonist* published an article about a railway crewmember who found a "half man and half beast" creature on the tracks. "Jacko," as the beast was later called, had long black hair, was 1.4 metres in height and weighed about 58 kilograms. He resembled a human but had extra-long forearms, and his entire body, except for his hands (or paws), was covered with 2.5-centimetre-long hair. Unfortunately, Jacko died before he could be exhibited or studied further.

## The Merman

The century-old Indian Trading Post in Banff, Alberta, is home to the store's most famous resident, the Merman. Is it actually the physical remains of a half-human, half-fish creature? While the Merman looks suspiciously like a monkey skeleton head and torso fused onto a fish's rear, it is supposedly of "unknown origin," so we'll leave it there. Don't forget to buy a postcard of this creature posing against one of Banff's stunning glacial lakes. Postcard: one dollar. The look on your friends' faces when they open their mail: priceless.

# What Lies Beneath

Was it an otter? A beaver? A previously thought-to-be-extinct plesiosaur? How about a log bobbing up and down on the water's surface? Step aside Nessie: Canada has some stiff competition for you, and many of our creature sightings predate any Scottish tourist monster. Dracontology is the study of dragon and serpent-like creatures, and there are plenty here in Canada to ponder:

*Caddy and Amy:* According to Native folklore, a serpentine creature has always inhabited Cadboro Bay, BC, but modern sightings were first documented in the 1920s. In 1933, this 18-to-20-metre-long creature with two large flippers, slender neck and camel-like head was given the name "Cadborosaurus," or "Caddy" for short. A similar, yet smaller, version named "Amy" is believed to be Caddy's mate. The two may have even produced baby Cadborosauri, since a few unusual eel-like creatures resembling the parents have also been spotted by fishermen.

*Champ:* The creature dubbed "Champ" is a Loch Ness Monster look-alike that swims in the depths of Lake Champlain in Québec (bordering on New York and Vermont). A famous photo of the mythical monster surfaced in 1997, along with an account by an eyewitness who described seeing "the head come up…then the neck, then the back."

*Igopogo:* First reported in the early 1950s, Igopogo is Lake Simcoe's very own legendary creature. He, or she, is greyish in colour, between 10 and 20 metres long and sports fins (but no word if it also wears goggles).

*Kingstie:* Reports of "Kingstie" go back at least as far as 1867. This serpent lives in the St. Lawrence River near Kingston, Ontario, and apparently raced a steamer in 1881.

*Manipogo:* This olive-green serpent was first spotted in Lake Manitoba but has been known to travel by waterways to other lakes in the province. The community of St. Laurent, Manitoba, celebrates a Manipogo Festival each March, but the shy monster has yet to turn up for the party.

*Memphré:* Like Loch Ness, Lake Memphremagog—between Magog, Québec, and Newport, Vermont—is a deep, long lake with a sea monster resident. "Memphré" is black, 10 to 12 metres long, with humps, webbed feet and possibly horns or tusks. The creature has been sighted over 200 times in the last century and is described in the novel, *The Sea Serpent Legend*, by Norman Bingham, written in 1926:

*They saw a monster dark and grim*
*Coming with coiling surge and swim*
*With lifted head and tusk and horn*
*Fierce as the spirit of Hades born.*

*Old Ned:* Lake Utopia in southern New Brunswick reportedly harbours a huge monster approximately 30 metres in length. One legend claims the creature chased Aboriginal peoples in a canoe with its "bloody jaws." Nicknamed "Old Ned," the serpentine creature has frequently been sighted since at least 1842. He may simply be a large log or eel, but some believe Old Ned is an unknown species that migrates to the Atlantic through deep canals and returns to Lake Utopia every few years.

*Ogopogo:* Since the late 1700s, there have been thousands of sightings of "Ogopogo," the serpentine creature that may inhabit Okanagan Lake, BC. Native lore of *Naitaka* or *N'ha-ha-itq*, as it was called, go back even farther, and the monster is depicted with the head of a sheep or a horse on ancient petroglyphs. In 2001, a $2-million reward was offered for concrete proof of Ogopogo. While grainy photographs and even a film taken in 1968 do exist, no one has yet claimed the hefty prize. What's more,

Ogopogo has been granted protected wildlife status under legislation enacted by the Province of British Columbia in 1989. It is now illegal to harm, kill, capture or disturb any endangered species, including the Ogopogo.

*Ponik:* Lake Pohenegamook, near the Québec border with Maine, is home to Ponik, the lake's monster. Sightings of Ponik were first documented in 1874 and hundreds of times since. A priest fishing on the lake in 1957 claimed he actually saw the 10-metre-long, black, humped creature before it disappeared under the water.

# Hertz 52

Why not try hunting for Hertz 52 instead? Of no relation to the famous Heinz 57 sauce, Hertz 52—actually 51.75—is a frequency similar to the one just above the lowest note on a tuba. Hertz 52 has been heard since 1989 along the North Eastern Pacific coast, but no one can pinpoint what or where it is coming from. Maybe it is a whale, but it doesn't match the frequency of any known whale species and even seems to be getting lower over time. It could be a deformed whale, or maybe the last of an unknown species, destined to call for years but never to receive a reply....

# CRAZY OLYMPICS

*Canadians love their sports. From alpine skiing to wrestling, baseball to football, lacrosse to dog sled racing, we take our games super seriously and in the strangest ways. Ever tried to find a show on television worth watching, besides hockey, during playoff season? Point made.*

## Olympic Trials

Higher, Stronger, Faster. How about Wilder, Weirder, Wackier? Canada has a peculiar history with the Olympics. First, we got off to a slow start. Canada didn't really join the Olympics until 1904 and only sent our first official team in 1908. Then it took over five long decades until we actually got a gold medal—for rowing in 1964. Secondly, we had a hard time keeping up with the high athletic pace. In 1968, Canada only won one gold medal, and even that was with the help of three horses in equestrian events.

Our luck finally changed when Montréal hosted the games in 1976. After losing out in 1972, Mayor Jean Drapeau wasn't going to let the next Olympics slip by. A new stadium would be built, he declared, at a cost of $124 million. The Olympic Stadium, the "Big O," turned out to be the "Big Owe" when the final bill came to $1.5 billion—Montréal's Olympic-sized debt took 18 years to pay off. In 1988, Canada got another chance with the Winter Olympics in Calgary, and most recently in Vancouver 2010. Maybe with global warming, we'll one day be able to host a Summer Olympics....

### Who Messes Up Better Than Lastman…Nooobody!

Mel Lastman, the Toronto mayor and former furniture salesman (who famously went to the Arctic in the 1960s to "sell a refrigerator to an Eskimo"), found himself in hot water after an Olympic gaffe. Lastman was on his way to Kenya to lobby for Toronto's 2008

Games Bid but ended up speaking too soon. "What the hell do I want to go to a place like Mombassa?" Lastman said to the press. "I'm sort of scared about going there, but the wife is really nervous. I just see myself in a pot of boiling water with all these Natives dancing around me." Lastman later apologized, but to the International Olympic Committee members, it raised serious questions about the Canadian delegation. His derisive comments about Africans created a stir, and Toronto subsequently lost the bid to Beijing.

## The Relay to End All Relays

Over 12,000 Canadians were chosen to carry the Olympic Torch across Canada in the longest torch relay ever, during the Vancouver 2010 Olympic Winter Games. Among the celebrity torchbearers was the 1988 Olympian skier, and loser,

Eddie the Eagle (hey, he's not Canadian!), ex-Olympian runner Sebastian Coe (hey, he's also not Canadian!) and the Austrian-born, California governor, Terminator and former Mr. Olympian, Arnold Schwarzenegger (he's *definitely* not Canadian!). Torchbearers were given the option of forking out $400 to purchase their Bombardier-made torch (which resembled a giant barbeque lighter) after the event. A few torches had been signed by singer Céline Dion, who had made an appearance on the assembly line. Her autograph may have made the purchase worth the money (or not, depending on whom you ask).

## Tourist Tips

With a budget of $900 million for security, paid for by the federal government, Vancouver 2010 organizers didn't take any chances. According to the Olympic Resistance Network (an anti-Olympic protest group), at least three U.S. activists were turned away at the border and not allowed to enter Canada. Hey, they couldn't have been *that* crazy since they actually knew where Vancouver, Canada, was located. Several tourists reportedly tried to make hotel reservations in Vancouver, Washington, unaware that it was the *other* city of Vancouver that was hosting the Games.

Okay, perhaps we take our clean water for granted. Officials had to assure visiting athletes and foreign tourists that it was perfectly okay to drink Vancouver tap water.

# Let the Games Begin

It was a rough start. Only hours before the opening ceremonies, a Georgian luge athlete named Nodar Kumaritashvili lost control of his sled while going 150 kilometres per hour and flipped over the barricades, slamming into a metal support pole. His tragic death cast a pall over the start of the Games. On the first day of events, police also arrested several rebel anti-Olympic

protestors for smashing windows of the downtown Hudson's Bay store, a huge Games supporter. Another big problem was the warm, balmy weather, and organizers had a major headache keeping enough snow on the slopes. There were other glitches and criticisms: British media dubbed the Vancouver Olympics the "Calamity Games," and a Montréal newspaper ran the headline "French as Rare as Snow in Vancouver" to protest the lack of French-speaking volunteers in Vancouver. Perhaps the weirdest comment was made by a Swiss radio interviewer, who asked an Olympic committee official why they permitted the Games to be held in a coastal region with such a "Caribbean" climate. We wish!

### Colbert's Canadian Connection

Stephen Colbert, or at least his character on television, has a habit of putting down Canadians, and no more so than during the Vancouver Olympics. When the U.S. speed-skating team faced a $300,000 shortfall in their budget after a corporate sponsor pulled out because of the recession, Colbert publicly came to their rescue. He drummed up funds from fans of the *Colbert Report* television show and went on to defend Team USA, calling Canadians "syrup-suckers" and "iceholes" in the process. But, when a Canadian genealogy website found out that Colbert's great-great-grandfather had immigrated to Ontario from Ireland in the 1880s, the tables were turned. Colbert admitted he believed it could be true, but added, "I'm not sure my character does."

## Stayin' Around

A spokesperson for Immigration Canada stated that 22 people involved with the 2010 Olympics made refugee claims to remain in Canada. Claimants came from such countries as Ghana, Hungary, Russia and even Japan (apparently the latter wasn't seriously considered). The number, though, was smaller than other sporting events. After the 1994 Commonwealth Games in Victoria, BC, 730 refugee claims were filed.

### Better Than an Olympic Medal?

It may not be an official Olympic sport, but with sold-out hotels and thousands of extra tourists, odds are there was a lot of "extra-curricular" calorie-burning activities taking place in Vancouver during the Winter Olympics. Jumping on the bandwagon, a local East Vancouver "adults-only" store offered a 10-percent discount to Olympic ticket holders. Olympic media personnel were given a five-dollar coupon and a free sex toy guide, and athletes who won an Olympic medal received a free vibrator. A Vancouver Olympic media relations spokesperson said the committee "respectfully declines the opportunity to comment."

# In Canada, Hockey Comes First

The gold medal game between Canada and the U.S. in the Vancouver 2010 Winter Olympics was definitely a nail-biter. So much so that passengers waiting to board an Air Canada flight from Vancouver didn't want to take their eyes off airport televisions despite repeated boarding announcements. An Air Canada executive said the reason for the delay was one they had "not yet encountered in over 72 years of existence." Canada finally beat their rivals 3–2 with an overtime goal by fan favourite Sydney Crosby, and the fans finally, and happily, boarded their flight.

# FOOTBALL FEVER

*Question:* *Why does American football have the rules it does?*
*Answer:* *They copied the Canadians.*

## Will the Real Football Game Please Stand Up

No, this is not a joke. It actually happened during a friendly game between two universities—Montréal's McGill and Boston's Harvard—in 1874. Although soccer and rugby were the main "foot" sports at the time, Harvard and McGill met up for a different kind of two-game exhibition series. One game used Harvard's rules and a round ball, while the other used McGill's rules and a pointed ball. After the first game began, the Harvard players much preferred McGill's version, which allowed picking up and running with the ball, and they agreed to play the second match that way, too. The series ended in a scoreless tie, but Harvard came away with a great deal of admiration for the "Canadian" rules.

### Crazy Grey Cups

The Grey Cup, named after Governor General Earl Grey, is the famous East versus West showdown for the Canadian Football League's (CFL) ultimate prize. The silver trophy itself only cost the grand sum of $48 to make. Designed by Birks Jewellers in London, England, it didn't arrive in time for the first Grey Cup game on December 4, 1909, between the Toronto Parkdales and the University of Toronto. The Cup has since been present at all subsequent Grey Cup games, even if Mother Nature did her best to prevent a handful of them:

*The Cold Bowls:* On December 4, 1926, the Grey Cup was played in Toronto's Varsity Stadium, but the weather was so cold that the field turned to ice and the football froze solid. A riot broke out when fans tried to obtain refunds, but the box office happened to be closed. The game held in November 1975 was one of the coldest Grey Cups ever. The temperature in Calgary was at least −30°C with the wind chill. Despite the conditions, Edmonton won 9–8 over Montréal on the frozen AstroTurf.

*1939 Snow Bowl:* During the Grey Cup game in Ottawa, heavy snow began to fall. Winnipeg eventually went on to beat the Ottawa Rough Riders 8–7, but snow squalls had made visibility so poor that any vehicles parked along the sidelines had to leave their headlights on just so everyone could see the field.

*1950 Mud Bowl:* Warm temperatures mixed with 25 centimetres of snowfall the day earlier created a recipe for intense mud at Varsity Stadium in Toronto. No one could kick properly, and tackled players slid up to eight metres in the muck. At one point, the 27,000 fans even thought a linesman who was lying prone in the mud had drowned. The Toronto quarterback resorted to taping thumbtacks to his fingers so he could grip the ball better. It likely helped as Toronto went on to beat Winnipeg 13–0.

*1962 Fog Bowl:* The fog at Exhibition Stadium in Toronto was so thick that spectators in the upper stands couldn't see a thing on the field. Even television broadcasters admitted they had no idea "what was going on down there." The game was finally stopped with nine minutes left and was resumed the next day. Less than half the usual spectators turned out to watch Winnipeg eventually triumph over Hamilton 28–27.

*1965 Wind Bowl:* Wind gusts up to 80 kilometres per hour at Exhibition Stadium in Toronto meant players trying to punt saw the ball actually fly backwards. Of the 60 minutes to be played, 50 were in the east end of the stadium. Luckily, they switched sides after halftime, but Hamilton still defeated Winnipeg 22–16.

*1971 Swamp Bowl:* In Vancouver, the Argos went slip sliding away and lost to Calgary 14–11 on a totally waterlogged field. It had become like a grassy sponge after six days of heavy rain.

## One Tough Prize

The Grey Cup has been broken on several occasions by overexcited celebrants, and three of those times were by the Edmonton Eskimos, including one incident in 1987 when a player sat on it. In 1928, the Hamilton Tiger Cats won it, but their manager forgot it in a closet for a year. In 1947, a fire destroyed the Toronto Argonaut Rowing Clubhouse where the Grey Cup was being stored. It fell off a shelf but fortunately snagged on a nail, thereby preventing it from falling into the flames.

### The Hostage Cup

In 1969, just before Christmas, the Grey Cup was stolen from its display case in Ottawa. A ransom letter left at the scene demanded cash, but CFL officials refused. After a few mysterious phone calls in early January 1970, the CFL just decided to make a replica and said if the original was ever returned, it would be preserved in the Hall of Fame. By mid-February, another anonymous call to police indicated where the trophy could be found, stashed in a locker at an Ottawa hotel. The trophy was back, but a replica was still made in 1972 for $550, plus tax, which was more than the cost of the original trophy anyway.

# Pamela's Wave

Famous buxom actress Pamela Anderson was discovered at a CFL game in July 1989. A cameraman caught her doing "the wave" in a Labatt T-shirt. Featured on the Jumbotron, she was asked to draw the winning 50–50 ticket and, after the game, was hired by Labatt's to star in an upcoming ad. One thing led to another, including a *Playboy* shoot, a starring role on the *Baywatch* series and finally celebrity status, all thanks to her being a Canadian football fan. Guys, tell your girlfriends.

## Famous Fumble

A famous photo was taken by Doug Ball of the Canadian Press on May 30, 1974. It depicts Conservative Leader Robert Stanfield fumbling a football during a relaxing game of catch in the middle of his federal election campaign. The *Globe and Mail* newspaper ran the photo with the headline, "Political Fumble?" Whether or not it altered voters' opinions is debatable, but it sure made Stanfield look incompetent, at least when it came to football. Pierre Trudeau later won the election with a majority.

# THE HOCKEY NEWS

**Question:** *What do you get when you cross a groundhog with a Maple Leaf player?*
**Answer:** *Six more weeks of bad hockey.*

–Old Maple Leafs Joke

## Dropping the Puck

Windsor, Nova Scotia, likes to call itself the birthplace of hockey. In 1789, young men from Kings College played "hurley," an Irish sport, on ice and added rules from both cricket and the Mi'kmaq version of an ice game to create hockey. In effect, hockey is a strange mixture of shinny, field hockey, hurley and cricket. The game really started to take on its own form when the rubber puck was invented in 1872 and the first indoor hockey rink opened in Montréal. Now, *that's* hockey.

## Stanley Cup

It's the oldest professional sports trophy in North America, bought in London in 1892 by Lord Stanley of Preston. Nicknamed the "Stovepipe Cup" because of its ringed appearance, the Stanley Cup is the three-foot-tall holy grail of hockey. But surely it can't be *that* sacred, especially when you consider what it's been through. It was lost in 1924 when the Montréal Canadiens inadvertently left it by the side of the road after changing a flat tire. Fortunately, they returned to find it still sitting in the same spot. It was stolen in 1961 when a Canadiens fan broke into its case in Chicago after the Blackhawks won. His excuse? He said he was simply going to take it back to Montréal, where it belonged. It has also been used as a toilet when, in 1964, Toronto Maple Leaf Red Kelly had a picture taken with his baby son sitting in the Cup, only to find out later the infant had peed in it. It has been used as a baptismal font, and, thanks to a racy photograph taken in Edmonton in the mid-1980s, we know at least one stripper has treated it like a dancing pole. Enough said.

# Engraved Forever

The stories behind the Stanley Cup are as numerous as the names etched into it. Many of those names are misspelled—just ask Jacques Plante, or would that be Jac, Jacq or Jaques Plante? There is also the case of the oddly placed name of Harry "Punch" Broadbent. Although Broadbent is mentioned on the first ring along with his Montréal Maroons teammates who won in 1926, his name also appears upside down, and strangely alone, along the outer ring of the bowl. No one really knows why. Another name has been glaringly crossed out. When the Edmonton Oilers won it in 1984, the owner, Peter Pocklington, gave a list of all players and team members to be engraved on the Cup. He surreptitiously included his dad's name, Basil, even though the senior Pocklington had no official position on the team. Furious, NHL executives later ordered the engraver to put x's

through each letter of Basil's name. At least they didn't write "Ass Man" after his name, which is what they did in 1945 to denote the team's ASSistant MANager, Frank Selke. His team? The later-misspelled Toronto Maple Leaes, of course.

### Clear the Track…For This Nose
Canadian hockey player Eddie Shack was nicknamed "The Entertainer," "Pugnacious Pinocchio" and "The Nose" for his prominent proboscis. He was featured on commercials in which he'd quip, "I have a nose for value."

# Death Brawls

*I went to a fight last night and a hockey game broke out.*

–Old Canadian joke

Whether you stand up and cheer or turn away in disgust, those non-Olympic hockey games often have fights. During a hockey game in 1905, Allan Loney of Maxville, Ontario, pummelled opponent Alcide Laurin with his stick—Laurin never regained consciousness, and Loney was charged with manslaughter. He pleaded self-defence and was later acquitted. In 1907, Charles Masson, a player with the Ottawa Vics, was charged with manslaughter after Owen McCourt, a Cornwall player, died after being struck over the head with a stick. Masson was later acquitted when it became unclear whether or not it was actually his stick that killed McCourt. In January 2009, Don Sanderson, a 21-year-old player with the Whitby Dunlops, died after a hockey fight in which his helmet came off and he fell to the ice on his head.

## Sad Endings

On December 12, 1970, Brian Spencer, a player with the Toronto Maple Leafs, was to be interviewed during the intermission on the CBC's *Hockey Night in Canada*. Back home in Fort St. James, BC, Brian's father, Roy, tuned in to watch his son but discovered the television station was airing the Vancouver-Oakland game instead of the Toronto-Chicago one. Furious, Roy snapped, grabbed a rifle and drove two hours to the CBC studios in Prince George, where he forced employees to cut the transmission. The RCMP arrived, and Roy was killed during the subsequent shootout. Despite the tragedy, Brian continued to play for the NHL until 1979. He fell in with the wrong crowd and, in 1987, faced a murder charge but was acquitted. About to start rebuilding his life, Brian was unfortunately shot and killed by a robber three months later.

# *That's* ONE CRAZY CANUCK!

## Mr. Tactless, Don Cherry

Don "Hot Lips" Cherry? It's a fitting moniker for one of hockey's most outspoken and outlandish *Hockey Night in Canada* commentators. He earned the nickname on May 19, 1993, when he kissed NHL player Doug Gilmour during the playoffs. Millions of viewers didn't seem to mind. They cringed instead at his outlandish, drapery-inspired, custom suits he wears during *Coach's Corner* and the eccentric remarks he spouts for seven minutes while sitting next to his character-foil co-host, the ever-polite Ron MacLean. Even though Don Cherry only played one game in the NHL—in 1955 for the Boston Bruins—he ended up as the head coach of the Bruins, where they gained their reputation as a tough team. Cherry's "rock 'em, sock 'em" stance toward hockey has not only attracted millions of fans but has also generated lots of controversy with concerns that it promotes hockey violence.

But Cherry is no stranger to criticism or to speaking his mind. His remarks have infuriated many people, including CBC executives, European players, Russians, those against the war in Iraq—you name it, he's infuriated it. In 2006, he was booed by Bloc Québecois MPs for saying that French Canadian players weren't as tough as other players. Despite his brazenly big mouth and conservative views, Cherry doesn't hesitate to support charitable causes. When his long-time wife, Rose, died in 1997, Cherry established the Rose Cherry Home for Sick Children. In 2004, he made it to the top 10 as one of the

"Greatest Canadians" as chosen by CBC viewers. But it's hockey that Cherry lives for. In his own words, "I don't have any hobbies. I don't golf. I don't fish. I have no other interest in life except hockey. I wake up in the morning thinking about it, and go to bed thinking about it." And every Saturday night during hockey season, he tells us exactly what he thinks about it.

# Keep It Going

The longest game ever played in the NHL was on March 24, 1936, during the Stanley Cup playoffs. After six (yawn) overtime periods, 176 minutes and 30 seconds of play, Detroit finally beat Montréal. As extraordinary as that game was, it was nothing compared to what 39 Alberta hockey players later accomplished. Between February 8 and 18, 2008, they gathered at an outdoor rink just east of Edmonton and raised over $500,000 for pediatric cancer research by playing the longest hockey game in the world. They skated, checked, passed and scored for a staggering 240 hours—that's 10 straight days—in temperatures ranging from 0°C to –40°C with the wind chill. Team Cure eventually triumphed over Team Hope by a score of 2250–2223, but no one was really keeping track.

## Masked Men

The first goalie in the NHL to wear a face mask was actually Clint Benedict of the Montréal Maroons. After his nose was broken by a shot from Howie Morenz, Benedict donned a mask for the 1929–30 season. It was Jacques Plante, the gifted Montréal Canadiens goalie, however, who became the first to regularly wear the mask. Off-ice, Plante had another talent: knitting.

# PLAY BALL

*Canada is a country whose main exports are hockey players and cold fronts. Our main imports are baseball players and acid rain.*

–Pierre Trudeau

## Baseball, the Canadian Game

Our American friends like to think that baseball was "invented" by Abner Doubleday in Cooperstown, New York. Not so fast. A letter published in *Sporting Life* magazine in 1886 makes reference to a game remarkably similar to today's baseball, but it was played a full year before the Cooperstown event. Dr. Adam Ford, who grew up in the small town of Beachville, near London, Ontario, wrote of a game played on June 4, 1838, between two teams, the Beachville Club and the Zorras. Ford's detailed documentation of the match makes it the first record of a formal baseball game in North America.

### Flag Flap

No, it wasn't a distress signal, although the Toronto Blue Jays were probably feeling the pressure after losing game one of the 1992 World Series to Atlanta. It was October 18, 1992, and both teams were ready for pre-game ceremonies at the stadium in Atlanta. As per usual, the U.S. Marine Corps raised the flag of both countries during their national anthems. But even before Tom Cochrane could sing "O Canada, we stand on guard" twice (which he mistakenly did), some eyebrows were already raised. Oops! The Canadian flag was flying upside down! Apologies gushed from the Corps and game officials. The Blue Jays ended up winning game two, and when the series resumed in Toronto a few days later, the Corps requested the privilege of making amends. A Marine guard presented the Canadian flag again, no small gesture since Marines are usually prohibited from carrying the flags of other nations. Canadian fans applauded loudly to show there were no hard feelings, although a few homemade "We Won in 1812, too" and "The Right Way, Eh?" banners appeared among the crowds. Hey, mistakes do happen, and it was, after all, the first World Series ever played outside the United States. Our national pride wasn't bruised, and we went on to win the series to boot, although one wonders if the situation had been reversed—what if we had accidentally flown the American flag upside down? Whoa!

## Baskets of Fun

Every August, the village of Almonte, Ontario, closes its streets and has baskets of fun during the Naismith 3-on-3 Basketball Festival in honour of their hometown hero and basketball's inventor, James Naismith.

# FUN 'N' GAMES

*We'll explain the appeal of curling to you, if you explain
the appeal of the National Rifle Association to us.*

–Andy Barrie

## Ice Canoeing

Want to do a real man's sport? One that's so tough and treacherous that it's only found on the wintry St. Lawrence River? How
about ice canoeing? What supposedly began as a competition for
those who wanted to be awarded the contract to deliver the mail
has turned into dangerous annual races for those willing to brave
strong currents and floating hunks of ice. Ice canoe races are
a highlight of the famous winter festival, the Carnival de Québec.

### It's a Toss-up

Don't be surprised if you see someone bouncing up and down
on a large blanket in Canada's most northern town of Inuvik.
The blanket toss, or *nalukatuk*, is a traditional game whereby
a large group of people grasp the edges of a stretched blanket,
about three metres in diameter, and toss a participant high into the
air. Often played at festivals and other Inuit celebrations—it was
demonstrated when the Olympic Torch made its way through
Inuvik in January 2010—the blanket toss has its roots as a hunting ritual. The bouncer was usually someone with good eyesight
who, when bounced high enough, could spot game in the distance. Originally made from seal or walrus skin, most blankets
today are canvas. Good bouncers can reach up to 10 metres
high, and when Governor General Michaëlle Jean gave it a try
during a northern visit, she made it an impressive four metres
into the air.

## Surf's Up...in Montréal

Who says you can't surf in Montréal? Grab a board and surf a standing wave in the Lachine Rapids right behind the Habitat '67 housing complex in the city. Former Olympic kayaker (he represented South Africa in the 2002 Olympics) Corran Addison can show you how. He started up what is now the biggest river surfing school in Canada. Each year, over 800 students learn to "hang ten" during two-day lessons, which include a board, life jacket and helmet rental. While the St. Lawrence River isn't exactly the ocean (try to not swallow the water!), thanks to underground boulders, waves can reach up to two metres high, enough to thrill any surfer. In the winter, Corran and his friends have even ice-surfed, but dodging ice floes is definitely not for the timid. In the summer, the surfing is great, even if you're 500 kilometres away from the nearest beach.

### Game Over

Move over, HAL, there's a new computer king out there. When it comes to the game of checkers, Chinook will beat any human, any time. The computer program—developed in the early 1990s by University of Alberta computer science professor, Jonathan Schaeffer—even beat the world checkers champion in 1994.

No small feat considering he had only lost nine games in 40 years of competition. In 2007, Chinook's creators made an announcement. With the help of Chinook, they had solved the game of checkers. Play the game with Chinook, and eventually you will lose or, if you're as smart as a computer, end in a draw. And like tic-tac-toe, checkers can end in a draw again, and again, again....

## Small Balls, Only in Canada, Eh?

If those 10-pin bowling balls are simply too heavy for you, thank a Canadian for creating the alternative. In 1908, Thomas Ryan of Toronto had the first 10-pin bowling alley in Canada, the Toronto Bowling Club. With its palm tree décor and string orchestra, the elite club resembled a southern plantation. The game grew in popularity, but players complained that the 16-pound bowling balls were way too heavy. Ryan decided to create a lighter ball, use fewer pins and make them three-quarters smaller, and voilá, five-pin bowling was invented. Like 10-pin, the aim is to knock over the pins, though the scoring is slightly different. It's only played in Canada, though—pity, eh?

### Tub Racing

Most of us fill our bathtubs with water so we can enjoy a nice, relaxing soak. Every July in Nanaimo, BC, however, you'll find crazed competitors speeding their suped-up motorized tubs around a racecourse just off the coast. The Loyal Nanaimo Bathtub Society has held the International Bathtub Race since 1967, and it's the most famous one in the world (New Zealand and the U.S. also have bathtub races—thank goodness we're not the only zany country to embrace this "sport").

## School Fights

On August 26, 2008, 900 students from Ryerson University in downtown Toronto battled with blue plastic swords for 12 minutes.

Their melee, which was part of orientation week activities, went down in the record books as the largest one-time sword fight.

**Big Games**

*Chauvin, Alberta—World's Largest Softball:* Made in 1977 and measuring 1.8 metres in diameter, Suzie the giant softball has a painted-on smile that could melt a ping pong ball. Too bad the World's Largest Aluminum Bat in Edmonton hasn't met her yet—the two might really hit it off.

*Duncan, BC—World's Largest Hockey Stick and Puck:* Known as the "Totem Pole Capital" for its 80-plus totem poles, this Vancouver Island city won a competition to display a 62.5-metre-long stick (and puck) used in Vancouver's Expo '86. Duncan has since been referred to as the "Little Town That Pucked Up."

*Houston, BC—World's Largest Fly Fishing Rod:* If you love fly fishing, then get thee to Houston, BC. You'll find this small town situated between Prince Rupert and Prince George. Just look for the giant 20-metre-long rod and be prepared to catch abnormally large steelhead fish.

# EAT IN OR TAKE OUT

*Canada has never been a melting-pot; more like a tossed salad.*

–Arnold Edinborough

*From seal meat served raw to cod cheeks straight from Newfoundland, Canadian cuisine is more than meets the mouth. We have unique dishes to please, or at least perplex, almost every palate. Ever try moose muffle soup? It's boiled moose nose and lips, by the way. Not only can foodies relish in our specialties, but we like to honour our big country with big food, whether it's edible giant cheese or a fibreglass kielbasa. Throw in an oddball-shaped restaurant, and you've got a five-star meal you just can't get anywhere else in the world.*

## Dining in the Dark

For an out-of-sight dining experience, look no further than the O.NOIR restaurants in Toronto and Montréal. Guests order gourmet menu items such as spicy filet mignon, grilled octopus or chicken breast, but once seated, they're in complete darkness. Blind waiters easily navigate through the pitch-black room, but diners have been known to miss their plates or to use spoons to cut their food because they can't find their knife. It's a mere taste of what visually-impaired persons go through in their daily lives. The experience is guaranteed to be an eye-opener and will tantalize your tastebuds like nothing else.

Prince Edward Island's Potato Museum has a collection of diseased potatoes displayed in little coffins.

## Cowboy Cuisine

A restaurant in downtown Calgary, Buzzard's Cowboy Cuisine, holds a Testicle Festival during the annual Calgary Stampede. The famous dish is called "prairie oysters," also known as calves' testicles served fried, battered or boiled, with pasta or any way you like. The restaurant also sells T-shirts with catchy slogans such as "Having a Ball" and "Going Nuts."

# Giant Pepper Grinder

Would you like a little pepper on your entrée? Make that *a lot* of pepper. Dine at the Via Allegro Ristorante in Etobicoke, just outside Toronto, and you might do a double-take when you see the pepper grinder. At 3.6 metres tall, it almost touches the high ceiling and may just be one of the world's largest pepper grinders. To avoid the inevitable workplace accidents, waiters offer a much smaller version to flavour your meal.

## The Flying Saucer Restaurant

The Hershey Centre, a large sports arena in Mississauga, may look like a giant UFO built right off Highway 401, but if you

really want to check out a spaceship, try the breakfast special at the Flying Saucer Restaurant on Lundy's Lane in Niagara Falls, Ontario. The establishment is two saucers joined together to make one big eatery and take-out, complete with lights right out of a close encounters movie. The owner once offered a $1-million reward for anyone who could produce an actual UFO, or at least pieces of a real flying saucer, for his restaurant. Define "real," though. According to the offer, all material was to be submitted to labs and scientific centres for a complete analysis. In other words, there needed to be confirmation that it was extraterrestrial before any payment was made, but I wonder if a meteorite whittled into a little UFO shape would suffice?

# DRINK 'ER UP

*I* AM *CANADIAN*

–Molson's beer slogan

## A Loooong Brain Freeze

Winnipeg, Manitoba, holds the chilly title of "Slurpee Capital of the World." Yes, this frozen beverage that squirts out of a variety store dispenser like slush off a highway during spring thaw is a Winnipegger's favourite brain freeze. Since 1999, Winnipeg has topped Calgary and Detroit as the city with the most Slurpee sales. The mayor of the city even received an honorary Slurpee cup trophy. Surprisingly, the frozen drinks are consumed year round, even when it's –40°C outside.

### Bloody Good Drink

Beer may be Canada's favourite brew, but our national cocktail is the Bloody Caesar. We chug back around a quarter of a billion of the dark-red beverages annually. Bartender Walter Chell first made the drink in 1969 at the Calgary hotel where he worked. Like the Bloody Mary, he mixed vodka with tomato juice but added his own special ingredient—mashed clam juice. A British patron sipped the concoction and called it "a bloody good Caesar."

The name stuck, although if you try to order one anywhere but Canada, you'll probably get a strange look. Only in Canada again? Pity.

## Bloody Caesar Recipe
- *one ounce of vodka*
- *four ounces of Clamato juice*
- *two dashes of Worcestershire sauce*
- *celery salt*
- *two dashes of Tabasco sauce*
- *celery stalk*
- *lime wedge*
- *ice cubes*

Wet the rim of a tall glass with the lime wedge and dip into a saucer of celery salt. Add ice cubes to glass, followed by Worcestershire and Tabasco sauce. Stir, then add vodka and fill with Clamato juice. Stir once more and garnish with a celery stalk.

# The Stubby: R.I.P.

Mention the word "stubby" to boomers and their eyes will gloss over with fond, if not foggy, hangover memories. The stubby was Canada's compact beer bottle used as the industry standard from 1962 to 1983. It was replaced by the current, taller, American-style bottles for marketing reasons, despite the fact that ol' stubby was actually stronger and could be re-used more times than the longneck. The occasional stubby still turns up in old basements or garage sales. Take a whiff inside the bottle and chances are the musty beer smell still lingers, too.

## Drinks, Over Iceberg
It's pure, refreshing and easily over 15,000 years old. For less than $10, you too can have a chip off the old iceberg in your martini. Since icebergs are actually chunks of glaciers floating in the ocean, it's only natural that a few enterprising restaurants

in Newfoundland have tapped into this fresh ice supply. They collect "bergie bits," or ice pieces taken from icebergs, and chip them down for use in cool beverages. Icebergs usually melt by the middle of summer, so you might want to get a mini iceberg in your drink before then, while supplies last.

## Umm, There's a Sour Toe in My Drink

Dawson City, Yukon—a place where you can learn about the Klondike and famous gold rush of the late 1800s; where you can watch the Great International Outhouse Race; where you can read a book outside without a light at midnight in June; and not to mention a place where you can have a drink with a human toe in it. Yes, saunter into the Downtown Hotel, and, for five bucks, you can drink the infamous Sourtoe Cocktail and earn yourself a certificate for doing so. The tradition began in 1973 with a beer glass full of champagne and a vintage amputated miner's toe at the bottom. Today, you can have the toe with any beverage, but there is one cardinal rule: "You can drink it fast, you can drink it slow—but the lips have *gotta* touch the toe." The original sour toe is long gone (inadvertently swallowed—ewww!), but the bar is fully stocked with other donated human toes, all dehydrated and preserved in salt for your drinking pleasure.

### Got Milk?

When Dutch immigrant Jan Verdun arrived in Canada in 1930, he set to work as a farmhand and, by 1942, had saved enough money to buy his own feed mill in Alymer, Ontario. Verdun set up the first milk convenience store in March 1956, and he convinced a local glass manufacturer to fabricate three-quart jugs to hold the milk. Verdun's Dairy, as it was known, was open from 7:00 AM to 11:00 PM, seven days a week. In the early 1960s, a jug of milk and a pound of butter from the store cost a whopping one dollar.

# Plastic Udders

If you're from Ontario, Québec or the Maritimes, bagged milk is no big deal. If you're in western Canada or the United States, however, the idea of milk coming in those plastic udders can have a major "ewww" factor. Americans and their cartons or traditional quarts of milk find the bag as foreign as the word "serviette." A video on the Internet even went viral when it showed how Canadians (okay, make that *some* Canadians) drink milk, including a demonstration on how to snip the corner of the bag and pour the cow juice out properly. Other countries have embraced the plastic udders for years—South Africa, Argentina, Hungary and China, to name a few. The latter also bags beer, perhaps an idea we Canadians might one day embrace.

Plastic milk bags were actually introduced to Canada by the DuPont Company in 1967. When Canada went metric a decade later, the bag-making machines could be easily altered to cut one-litre-sized bags. Plastic jugs, on the other hand, involved a huge, expensive redesign of the equipment. Bags are also

considered "greener" because they use 75 percent less plastic.
By 1983, only the Becker's convenience store still carried the big
plastic jugs. It was eventually bought out by the Mac's chain,
where you can still find jugs on the shelf, right beside the
bagged milk.

# PECULIAR TASTES

*In any world menu, Canada must be considered
the vichyssoise of nations, it's cold, half-French and
difficult to stir.*

–Stuart Keate

## Heart Attack in a Bag

When a hurried customer walked into Fernand Lachance's restaurant in Warwick, Québec, in 1957, he asked for fries and cheese curds in a paper bag to go. Lachance replied the order would look like "a bloody mess" but sold it to him anyway for 35 cents. The mixture turned out to be more delicious than anyone in *La Belle Province* could've ever imagined, and poutine, a glorious mess of fries and cheese curds slopped in gravy, made Canadian food history.

### As Canadian as Mustard

Did you know Canada exports more mustard seed than any other country in the world, and 90 percent of it is grown in Saskatchewan? Yellow, brown and oriental mustard are used in many international condiment products, and most of our Canadian mustard seeds go to the United States, Belgium, Germany, Japan and the Netherlands. Something to think about the next time you reach for a jar of Dijon or squeeze that bright yellow stuff onto your hot dog.

## Easy on the Seal Meat

While polls suggest most Canadians would pass if offered seal meat, the main restaurant on Parliament Hill has added the northern staple to its weekly menu. In 2010, bacon-wrapped seal loin snacks were served to politicians and the media as a show of support from Canada's political parties regarding the controversial seal hunt. The European Union, on the other hand, has banned seal products from Canada and has condemned the annual hunt as inhumane.

### Soy, What?

Soy bean production is huge in Canada, with over 90 percent produced in Ontario alone. Ironically, most of this vegetable protein is shipped to Asia, where it is made into soy milk, tofu and that odoriferous fermented paste, miso.

Canadians eat more frozen French fries per person than people in any other country in the world.

# EXTRA HELPINGS

## Super-size That, Please

Make that a double, okay, a *quadrillion* scoop. The World's Biggest Sundae was created on July 24, 1988, at Palm Dairy in Edmonton and weighed almost 25 tonnes. Equally calorific was Canada's claim to one huge chunk of fudge. On May 24, 2007, the Northwest Fudge Factory in Sudbury made the World's Largest Slab of Fudge, a marbled white and dark chocolate confection weighing in at 2.29 tonnes. Local dentists were not impressed but appreciated the extra business.

### …And Hold the Fries

On May 7, 2010, Chef Ted Reader grilled a 268-kilogram beef patty in downtown Toronto to promote his latest barbeque cookbook. The monstrous hamburger (which was the equivalent of 2360 "normal-sized" burgers) took six hours to cook before it was placed in a 48-kilogram bun, topped off with sauce, lettuce, onions, tomatoes, pickles and sold for charity.

## Big Cheeses

Why are giant cheeses so appealing, especially in Canada? Take, for example, the southwestern town of Ingersoll and the site of the first cheese factory in Canada. In 1866, they made a 3310-kilogram round cheese to promote Canadian cheddar in Europe. The big cheese even crossed the Atlantic and made a huge splash in Liverpool, England. Almost three decades later, a 9980-kilogram cheese was churned out in Perth, Ontario. This massive dairy product, known as "The Canadian Mite," stood 1.8 metres tall and was 8.5 metres across. The cheddar travelled to the World's Fair in Chicago in 1893, where it was so heavy that it broke through the second-storey floor at the fair's Canadian pavilion. Perth was so proud of its mammoth cheese that it kept a 36-kilogram piece for its own museum and, in 1943, unveiled a full-sized concrete replica. In more recent cheese history, the Loblaws supermarket chain, along with a dairy in Granby, Québec, produced a colossal 26,900-kilogram cheese in 1995. It took 245 tonnes of milk to create the monster cheese and a specially-designed, 18-wheel refrigerated truck to transport it. The cheese toured Loblaws stores in Ontario and Québec before being cut up and promptly eaten.

**Plastic Food**

For those with an appetite for the bizarre, Canada has many inedible but just as tummy-turning humungous foods:

*Bow Island, Alberta—Pinto MacBean:* Besides the mega Pinto MacBean statue, this town also boasts the World's Largest Putter (for some not-so-mini mini golf), an oil derrick, a bean pot-shaped water tower and a giant steel sunflower. Too bad this town isn't in Texas; it would fit right in.

*Glendon, Alberta—World's Largest Pyrogy on a Fork:* Imagine a 2722-kilogram pyrogy on a fork, or see the real 7.6-metre-tall starchy one in Glendon's Pyrogy Park. The structure has been there since 1993, and every July, the townsfolk rally around it for their annual Pyrogy Festival.

*Mundare, Alberta—Giant Kielbasa:* What better way to celebrate the local meat-processing plant than a 12.5-metre-tall fibreglass kielbasa sausage coil? Sure, it cost $120,000 but think of all the kielbasa tourists it attracts.

*Oxford, Nova Scotia—Blueberry Man:* This town is called the "Blueberry Capital of Canada," so they created a giant smiling and waving blueberry as a tourist attraction. Makes sense to me.

*Vilna, Alberta—Mushroom Capital of Alberta:* You might think seeing a six-metre-tall mushroom means you need to cut back on your intake of those "other" kinds of mushrooms, unless you're in Vilna, Alberta, that is. The giant mushroom statues here are merely Vilna's way of celebrating these useful and historically important food fungi.

# BILL ME

*Tourists often comment that Canadian currency is among the most colourful in the world. We do like bright money, such as the mesmerizing blue hues on the five-dollar bill or subtle brown tones of the 100 (although, if you're like me, you rarely see those). But visitors must really wonder what we were thinking when they find out what we call our one-dollar and two-dollar coins. Because of the bird on one side, we nicknamed the dollar coin a "loonie," which to most sane people implies a crazed fanatic ready for a straitjacket and padded room—and "toonie" sounds right outta preschool. Yep, those are our unique Canadian coins alright. Got change for a pretty purplish 10?*

## Odd as a Three-dollar Bill

Between 1870 and 1935, Canadians used a 25-cent bill called a "shinplaster." We even had a three-dollar bill. It was eliminated in 1871, but a bank in New Brunswick continued to use them for another 15 years.

In 1685, the governor of New France was running short on cold hard cash so he paid his Québec troops with playing cards, with IOUs on the back!

### The Queen's Bad Hair Day

Look closely at a 1954 banknote, especially the area around the Queen's hair behind her ear. Is that, could it be, a devil's face? On closer inspection, a hooked nose, scary eye and mouth of a rather sinister figure does appear. While the commissioned engraver denied any deliberate mischief, these "Devil's Face" bills remained in production until the Bank of Canada changed the plates in 1956.

## Money to Burn

While the average $20 bill lasts about two years and the average $5 or $10 only half that, don't throw away those torn bills. If three-fifths are intact, the Bank of Canada says that bill is worth full value, and at least half the value if between two-fifths and three-fifths is left. A grid is used to calculate how much of the bill is left, but if you've got less than two-fifths, you're out of luck. What if your money went up in smoke? Save the ashes. For insurance purposes, it may be possible to determine the value and denomination of each bill.

### Plastic Money
The days of torn, ratty bills may be coming to an end—the Canadian government is on the verge of replacing the traditional cotton-based paper used to make bills with a nifty, high-tech polymer material that is more resistant to tearing and longer lasting. The new bills, which will be introduced into circulation during 2011, should be able to withstand several washes in denim jean back pockets as well.

## Canadian Ink on American Money

In 1857, Thomas Sterry Hunt, a chemistry professor at McGill University, invented a special chromium trioxide green ink. He sold the invention to the American government, who first used it on banknotes in 1862. The ink cannot be photocopied, destroyed or reproduced, but that hasn't stopped countless would-be fraudsters from trying. Perhaps if he had invented a purple ink instead, those U.S. bills would be nicknamed "purplebacks"?

### Flag Fears

Is there an American flag on older Canadian bills? Scrutinizing money handlers posed this unusual question shortly after these $2, $5 and $10 bills were introduced in the late 1980s. On close inspection, the flag atop the picture of the Parliament buildings looked remarkably like the American stars and stripes. Conspiracy theories aside, the answer was no, the flag was simply the Red Ensign, which was used in Canada before the Maple Leaf.

# CANADIAN COINAGE

## Lost Loonie?

Buddy, can you spare a voyageurie? Don't laugh, it could have happened in an alternate universe. The original design for the one-dollar coin actually had voyageurs and canoes on the front, but in November 1987, the master dies, which were on their way from Ottawa to the Winnipeg mint, mysteriously never arrived. Afraid that counterfeit thieves may have stolen the dies, officials chose a new design. This one pictured the famous loon, and the rest is history.

### Tonnes of Money

*Perhaps they should have depicted two deer on the toonie and called it "Two Bucks"?*

–Canadian money joke

No matter what our dollar is worth, we Canadians have a thing for big money. One is the giant replica of Canada's first gold coin in Virginatown, Ontario. For loonie fans, check out the large loonies in Echo Bay, Ontario, or Churchbridge, Saskatchewan. There's even a huge, 80-metre-high toonie in Campbellford, Ontario, just east of Toronto. Impressive, but perhaps not as famous as Sudbury's Big Nickel—that nine-metre-tall replica of a 1951 five-cent coin was built by artist Bruno Cavallo for the 1967 centenary and represents both Sudbury's mining history and Canada's nickel production. The city initially refused the giant nickel idea, but a local firefighter saved the day and helped raise $35,000 for the project. In May 2007, the Royal Canadian Mint in Ottawa produced the world's biggest gold coin. At 53 centimetres across and weighing 100 kilograms, the 99.9 percent pure gold coin is worth millions, especially at the current high price of gold.

# That's ONE CRAZY CANUCK! Put Me on a Stamp!

Charles Connell thought he had an attractive face. So much so that he decided to use a portrait of himself, not Queen Victoria, on a Canadian stamp. In 1859, the New Brunswicker, successful politician and postmaster general was instructed by the lieutenant-governor to design new one-, five-, 10- and 12.5-cent stamps. The colony was in the midst of changing from the old British pounds, shillings and pence currency to the cent and dollar, and the latest stamps were to be sold on May 1, 1860. When the lieutenant-governor opened a package of the new stamps mere days before the deadline, his jaw dropped. For some reason, Connell had put his own image on the five-cent stamp, the one used for domestic mail. While the other stamp denominations were acceptable, the Connell-faced stamp was declared invalid, and Connell soon resigned over the scandal.

A new postmaster general was named, and by July, the notorious five-cent stamp was replaced. Embarrassed by the ordeal, Connell bought up all 500,000 stamps decorated with his visage for about 31 pounds and burned them at his Woodstock, New Brunswick, home. Connell's political career bounced back, and he was eventually elected as the area's first Member of Parliament. As for the scandalous stamps, only a few sheets were kept as souvenirs, and it's believed that fewer than 50 are still around. If you find one, it could be worth thousands of dollars, but so far, no one has found a "postmarked" Connell five-cent stamp.

## Place Your Orders

Since it opened in 1908, the Royal Canadian Mint in Winnipeg has been making special coins for over 154 countries. Yes, the Mint makes kroners for Iceland, centavos for Cuba, pesos for Columbia and even a thousand-dollar coin for Hong Kong.

## Poppy Problems

In 2004, the Canadian mint produced 30 million specially designed quarters to honour Canada's war veterans. The 25-cent piece was the world's first coloured coin, with a pretty red poppy in the centre. It didn't take long before people noticed that the red paint on the poppy began to lighten and to chip when handled. The mint fixed the fading problem but was completely unprepared when another issue arose—government agents thought we were using the unusual coins to spy on Americans.

It all began when a few U.S. Army contractors travelling in Canada became suspicious of the new coins. One found a "poppy quarter" in the cup holder of his rental car and thought it might contain some sort of "nanotechnology." When put under a high-powered microscope, he reported to superiors that the centre appeared to have a "wire-like mesh" on top. Another agent found one of the quarters in his coat pocket. Was it surreptitiously planted there, and were Canadians spying on them? An espionage warning was apparently issued in early 2007, but the U.S. Defense Security Service later released a report saying it was issued in error and was based on false information. Sure, if I was afraid of a quarter, I wouldn't want to admit it either.

# YOU CALL THAT ART?

*When they said Canada, I thought it was up in the mountains somewhere.*

–Marilyn Monroe

*Our Canadian identity may be a little diverse, for lack of a better word, and not all our actors migrate south to make their fortune (okay, many do, but that's beside the point). But Canadian arts and entertainment are certainly unique. Sure, it's often controversial and frequently puzzling, but thankfully, it's never dull.*

## Voices of Rage

The National Gallery in Ottawa has quickly learned to repeat the mantra, "you can't please everyone." The issue this time was *Voice of Fire*, a large acrylic on canvas painting created by American painter Barnett Newman in 1967. The piece of "art" consisted of a vertical red stripe flanked by twin ultramarine blue stripes on either side, painted onto a huge 3.4-metre-by-2.4-metre canvas. It had hung at Expo '67 in Buckminster Fuller's geodesic dome, and no one had complained then. During the late 1980s, a Gallery representative asked Newman's widow (the artist died in 1970 at the age of 65) what she wanted for the painting. Mrs. Newman replied "whatever you think it's worth." The Gallery, with tax-payer funds in hand, forked out $1.8 million for the work, which understandably caused a media storm of controversy. Critics said that anyone with a paint roller could have made it, while art lovers pointed out its deeper meaning, and the Gallery went into defensive mode. In retrospect, *Voice of Fire* was probably a good deal given that a small grey-and-black ink-on-paper abstract by Newman sold for a cool $5 million in 2008.

## Flesh Dress

Is a meat dress in good taste? In 1987, Canadian artist Jana
Sterbak created an unusual work of art she called *Vanitas:
Flesh Dress for an Albino Anorectic.* The sculpture consisted
of 22 kilograms of raw, salted flank steaks sewn together as
a dress, hung on a mannequin and left to rot. Sterbak wanted
the piece to contrast vanity with mortality. In other words,
no matter what we do to make ourselves more beautiful, our
flesh will eventually decompose just like the meat dress. When
the artwork was displayed at the National Gallery in Ottawa,
protestors complained it was a waste of taxpayer money, not to
mention a waste of food.

## A Museum for Footsie Lovers

The Bata Shoe Museum in downtown Toronto should satisfy anyone with a fetish for beautiful, unusual and antique shoes. This unique, shoe-box-shaped museum was opened by the Bata Shoe Company in 1995, the same family company that was established in Canada in 1939 and also has a community in eastern Ontario named after it—Batawa. With an ever-increasing collection that now counts over 12,500 historic shoes and related objects, the museum lives up to its motto, "One Step at a Time." A current exhibit is called *Socks: Between You and Your Shoes* and features a 900-year-old sock from Egypt, stockings worn by Queen Victoria and a 13th-century pair of socks made from human hair.

# THAT'S ENTERTAINMENT

## This Show Really Is Bizarre

One of the most popular Canadian comedy shows of the early 1980s was *Bizarre*. Yes, that was its actual name. Hosted by John Byner, the show was full of outrageous sketches, gags and political satire. The episodes, which aired on CTV, were cleaned up for a PG audience, with any coarse language, bare breasts and nudity totally removed, unlike the original uncensored versions. One of the most popular skits spawned from *Bizarre* was the five-minute, incredible—albeit it very fake—"stunt-gone-wrong" featuring Super Dave Osborne, a bungling stuntman character played by comedian Bob Einstein. No matter how outrageous the spectacle (such as falling off the CN Tower) or how mangled or decapitated he became (the show went through dozens of mannequins), Super Dave always managed to give a thumbs up at the end of the stunt to show he was A-OK. The skit later spawned an entire *Super Dave* variety show that first aired in 1987.

### Cana-doh!

Was Homer Simpson Canadian inspired? There's definitely a Canada link since Matt Groening, the famous cartoon character's creator, said that his Saskatchewan-born father was the inspiration for Homer. Doh!

## Theatre New France

There's nothing like an entertaining play to keep the masses happy. On November 14, 1606, the settlement of Port Royal in today's Nova Scotia was the site of the first play ever staged in Canada and most of continental North America. It was a stellar production called *Le Théâtre de Neptune en la Nouvelle-France*, written and produced by Port Royal local, Marc Lescarbot. The performance was put on to welcome the return of their leader, Jean de Poutrincourt, and included such special effects as ship-to-ship cannon fire and coloured smoke bombs.

## The Great White North

Hoser, take off, belch, burp, fart—those were just the regular, everyday words from a short sketch on *Second City Television* that aired in the 1980s. For several minutes every episode, two unemployed brothers named Bob and Doug Mackenzie (played by Rick Moranis and Dave Thomas, respectively) argued about beer and anything else Canadian. Their skit was eventually turned into a full-length movie, *Strange Brew*, in 1983. While it may be hard to fathom, the plot was supposedly based on Shakespeare's *Hamlet*, except that in *this* version, the brothers are attempting to get free beer, and they fall into a series of bumbling adventures. It was a mindless movie, fer sure, but it certainly boosted the careers of Thomas and Moranis. They both later received the Order of Canada for their Canadian-based comedy. Beauty, eh?

# That's ONE CRAZY CANUCK! The Baron of Blood

Anyone who has seen a David Cronenberg movie might end up thinking, what kind of warped childhood did this sick puppy have? The truth is that Cronenberg had a fairly normal childhood. Born in 1943, he grew up in Toronto, read comic books and rode his bike. No weird stuff, yet. He originally studied science but changed to English and later went into film studies. Somewhere along the line, his brain began to produce very strange films indeed. It started with the psychologically dark *Stereo*, then developed into *Made Rabid*, which featured a porn star. Some people call his films overly offensive, with gory body distortions and weird sex scenes. We're not only talking about disturbing movies that purposefully shock audiences but also movies that pair "body horror" with intense psychological themes, putting images on screen that nobody has ever seen before, like a bloody VCR hole boring into the stomach of the main character in *Videodrome* (1983). The list goes on:

*Shivers* (1975): A murdered woman's dissolved organs are flushed down the drain, releasing a parasite into the plumbing, which turns other apartment dwellers into sex freaks.

*The Dead Zone* (1983): Based on the Stephen King thriller, this movie, starring Christopher Walken, was a little more "normal."

*The Fly* (1986): Cronenberg makes a cameo in this movie where Jeff Goldblum, playing an eccentric scientist, accidentally transforms himself into a half-human, half-fly creature.

*Dead Ringers* (1988): Jeremy Irons plays twin gynecologists who are perverted, drug addicted and use abnormal surgical instruments.

*Naked Lunch* (1991): Surreal objects, like freaky typewriters, turn into cockroaches.

*eXistenZ* (1999): Otherwise normal workers at a software company plug themselves into biomechanical videogame hardware and go berserk.

In 1978, a cache of more than 500 movies dating from 1903 to 1929 were found in the ground in Dawson City, Yukon, during a construction excavation. The 35-millimetre nitrate films had been perfectly preserved in the permafrost.

## Hairdresser to the Stars

Sydney Guilaroff was known as the man with the golden shears. Born in England in 1906, Guilaroff grew up in Winnipeg and Montréal before leaving for New York at the age of 14. As an apprentice barber, Guilaroff gave Louise Brooks—a starlet of silent films in the 1930s—her famous bob style when she patronized a salon where he was working. Guilaroff soon became the hairdresser to the stars and was the guy who dyed Lucille Ball's hair red, gave Claudette Colbert her bangs, got flown to Monaco to style Grace Kelly's wedding-day hair and even teased the tresses of such famous women as Elizabeth Taylor, Joan Crawford, Greta Garbo and Marilyn Monroe. According to Debbie Reynolds, "Guilaroff knew everyone and all their secrets…he was totally trustworthy."

Manhattan's Pizza Bistro and Music Club in Guelph, Ontario, staged the world's longest concert with multiple artists from November 4 to 12, 2006. The concert was 200 hours long with only five minutes for set-up in between performers.

## Canada's Strongman

Baby Cyprien-Noé "Louis" Cyr was born big, tipping the scales at over eight kilograms at birth in 1863. Although his father wasn't particularly huge, his muscular, six-foot-tall mother was often seen in the village of St. Cyprien, Québec, carrying large sacks of flour over her shoulders. By the time he was nine, Cyr weighed over 64 kilograms and could sling a calf over his back. With blond, Samson-like curly locks as a youth, Louis Cyr became well known for his incredible strength. At 18, he entered a strong-man competition and won it by lifting a horse completely off the ground. Cyr later married an attractive petite woman, Melina, who had also caught the interest of his rival, David Michaud. Michaud was known as the strongest man in Canada at the time, but Cyr easily defeated him by hoisting a 99-kilogram barbell with one hand; Michaud could only manage 72 kilograms.

Cyr gained success as he toured Québec and the northeastern U.S., setting records such as his one-hand dead lift of 124 kilograms and backlifting a platform holding 18 men, weighing over 1972 kilograms. He also performed in England before the Prince of Wales and 5000 spectators. In 1891, Cyr demonstrated his strength in Montréal when he famously restrained four draught horses, two on each side pulling hard in both directions. Swedish strongman August Johnson, whom Cyr beat in 1896, once said that "no man can defeat this elephant." Sadly, Cyr died of health complications at the age of 49, five years after his last match.

# The Great Farini

William Hunt was born in 1838 in Lockport, New York, not far from the famous Niagara Falls. At the age of five, rambunctious Bill moved to Port Hope, Ontario, with his Canadian parents. Unable to sit still for very long, he made his own tightrope wire and, by tying it between two chairs, practiced walking on it. Bill's father convinced his son to go to medical school, but before graduating, Bill secretly performed his first major stunt. Under the stage name, The Great Signor Farini, he walked blindfolded across a 150-metre rope strung between two buildings as 8000 spectators watched in amazement from below. Bill knew he wanted to be a tightrope walker more than he wanted to be a doctor, and one of the ultimate challenges he set for himself was traversing Niagara Falls. On August 11, 1864, the Great Farini crossed the brink of the Falls on stilts. When his competitor, a French daredevil called Blondin the Magnificent, walked across a tight-rope over the Falls while carrying a stove, Farini lugged a washing machine out on his back and did the laundry halfway across. Besides his outrageous high-wire stunts, Farini also invented folding theatre seats, parachutes and had a patent on his human cannonball act. The Great Farini died in Port Hope in 1929 at the age of 91, and the town later named a park after him.

# MUSICAL RIDES

## Woodstock? Nah, I'll Pass

Ah, the summer of 1969—free love and funny smoke filled the air, if you catch my drift. It was also when Woodstock, one of the most famous events in music history, took place. That year, Lighthouse was an up-and-coming Canadian rock band with an original jazzy sound. They were in New York City and scheduled to play at Woodstock, the now-well-known outdoor festival billed as "three days of peace and music." After thinking about it, the drummer and bandleader, Skip Prokop, said no thanks and backed out. Far too many people and far too little security was the reason he gave. Sprinkle a few drugs into the mix, maybe even into the water, and Woodstock might easily turn into a bad scene. It's not that Lighthouse didn't like playing festivals, Prokop explained years later. They did and played other major ones, including Atlantic City with 76,000 spectators and even the Isle of Wight festival in 1970, where Jimi Hendrix also performed. No, something about Woodstock gave the band a bad vibe. They backed out and, according to Prokop, "just stayed in New York and hung out that weekend." Over 400,000 people turned up at Woodstock, making it a defining moment in the hippie generation. Although Prokop realizes that playing Woodstock might have lifted the band "to mega-status," as he puts it, he has no regrets. With hits like "One Fine Weekend" and "Sunny Days," Lighthouse will none-theless always remain a musical beacon of the peace-and-love era.

### Captain Kirk's Record Career

In a warp-speed move, William Shatner, or Captain James T. Kirk as he's known from the wildly popular *Star Trek* series, made an album. Yes, it's a vinyl record straight from the late '60s with his face gracing the cover like he's a Queen rock star. The Montréal-born actor met a record producer while working on *Star Trek* and churned out *The Transformed Man* in 1968.

The spoken-word album contains famous songs recited by Shatner, such as "Mr. Tambourine Man" and "Lucy in the Sky with Diamonds," while music is playing in the background. In the album's liner notes, he refers to growing up in Canada and the fact that he and music are "old, familiar friends." Shatner released a follow-up spoken-word album in 2004 with the help of musician Ben Folds—the album was entitled *Has Been*.

## Sir Paul and the OPP

One of the many offbeat reasons behind the "Paul McCartney Is Dead" rumours of 1969 was the Ontario Provincial Police (OPP) badge worn by the Beatle on the band's *Sgt. Pepper's Lonely Hearts Club* album cover. The badge was apparently sent to McCartney by a Canadian fan, but most people around the world understandably had no idea what OPP meant. Because the last "P" in "OPP" is hard to make out, some thought the letters stood for OPD, or "Officially Pronounced Dead."

### Canadian Band Klaatu, or the Beatles in Disguise?

In 1977, *Rolling Stone* magazine named the band Klaatu "Hype of the Year," mainly because of a story that circulated several months earlier that suggested the band could actually be the Beatles reunited. The album *Klaatu*, produced by Capitol (the company that released the Beatles' records in the U.S.), didn't list any band members or songwriters, only the name, Klaatu. Klaatu was also the name of a character in the sci-fi movie *The Day the Earth Stood Still*, a film referenced on the cover art of a Ringo Starr album. Paul McCartney was also said to have uttered the words, "See you when the earth stands still" after a concert, and beetles (the bugs, not the band) are thought to be heard chirping at the start of the Klaatu song, "Calling Occupants of Interplanetary Craft." To top it all off, an American journalist who heard the album when it was released in 1976 said the single "Sub Rosa Subway" sounded just like the Beatles. In reality, Klaatu was a Canadian progressive rock band made up of musicians John Woloschuk, Dee Long and Terry Draper. They had no connection to the Beatles and always denied the rumours but certainly didn't mind all the free publicity.

## Give Peace…and Pot…a Chance

From all appearances, Suite 1742 at the Queen Elizabeth Hotel in downtown Montréal has been frozen in time—late May 1969, to be exact. Except for all the memorabilia now on the walls, not much has changed from decades ago when John Lennon and Yoko Ono used it to record "Give Peace a Chance" during their famous bed-in peace tour. Dozens of people, including Tommy Smothers, Timothy Leary, Petula Clark and members of a local Krishna temple, crammed into the room for the song, which was recorded in less than three hours. The bed-in and media frenzy lasted days longer, and during the couple's stay in Montréal, throngs of fans congregated outside the hotel. One 16-year-old girl convinced a security guard to let her and a friend in and even met with Lennon. The famous Beatle scribbled the lyrics to his song on a piece of cardboard and told her it would be worth something one day. She sold it an auction in 2008 for $830,000.

Another fan who met Lennon that week was 21-year-old Allan Rock. Rock later became a cabinet minister in Jean Chrétien's Liberal government and the Canadian Ambassador to the

United Nations, but back then he was just the idealistic president of the student union at the University of Ottawa. Hoping to arrange a meeting between Lennon and the Canadian prime minister, Rock travelled to Montréal and actually made contact with Lennon's manager. Two weeks later, Lennon and Ono arrived in Ottawa, and Rock drove them around in his Volkswagen. After Rock's sightseeing tour, they stopped to knock on the door of 24 Sussex, but then-Prime Minister Trudeau wasn't in, so Lennon left a note with the housekeeper. Trudeau finally met with the famous rock star and his wife when they returned to Ottawa six months later. The meeting was scheduled to fill a five-minute block but lasted for over an hour. No doubt, Trudeau and Lennon talked world peace and probably "pot" as well. Just days before the meeting, Lennon had given a secret testimony to a Canadian commission investigating marijuana laws. Lennon was against hard drugs but suggested that marijuana should be legalized. According to transcripts, he said Canada was the "only hope" for reformed marijuana laws and added that "Canada's image is just about getting groovy, you know."

## Cash the Cheque

Canadian-born actor Jim Carrey was a 10-year-old boy living in the suburbs near Toronto when he decided to mail in an application to work on *The Carol Burnett Show*. Carrey didn't get an interview, but he didn't give up. Before he was famous, Carrey wrote himself a post-dated cheque for $10 million. A decade later, Carrey was making millions as a successful actor.

### Elvis Sightings

Elvis Presley's only concert tour outside the United States was to none other than Canada. In early April 1957, the King of Rock 'n' Roll performed two concerts in Toronto and two in Ottawa. Fans travelled from as far away as Montréal (he wasn't allowed to play there due to his controversial on-stage gyrations) to see him.

The day after his Ottawa performance, eight female students from a local Catholic high school were expelled for having defied a school ban intended to "prevent corruption" by attending the concert. That August, Elvis played Vancouver. It was his last ever concert in a foreign country.

## Diamond Duping Dave

In 2008, the Ontario Provincial Police (OPP) pulled over a man speeding in Oakland, Ontario, near Brantford. The driver—who was wearing a silk scarf, alligator shoes and bore a striking resemblance to Van Halen frontman, David Lee Roth—said he indeed was the mega-rocker and was suffering from a nut allergy. A passenger in the car confirmed the story, and the OPP rushed "David" to a local hospital. After treatment, "David" posed for photographs with starstruck nurses and invited them to the nearest club, where he gave an impromptu rendition of "Ice Cream Man" with the local house band. Word quickly spread, and soon the entire incident made national and international news: famous rocker "saved" from anaphylactic shock by the OPP. Shortly thereafter, a few people recognized "David" and cried foul. He was a "David" alright, but a David who was a former drummer from Cambridge, Ontario, and not David Lee Roth, the zillionaire of "California Girls" fame. When contacted, the real David responded by saying he had been in Québec earlier that month for a concert but wasn't allergic to anything except criticism.

# That's ONE CRAZY CANUCK!

## Stompin' Tom Stomps Around

When CBC Television lost the rights to the popular theme music for *Hockey Night In Canada*, perhaps they should have considered Stompin' Tom Connors' famous "The Hockey Song." Virtually every Canadian who knows hockey has heard Connors' catchy tune. Connors was willing to talk about it, but CBC never called. No matter, Connors remains a cultural icon in this country with over 500 songs and 30 records to his name, including such hits as "Sudbury Saturday Night" and "Bud the Spud." Many of his songs are about the small rural towns he's performed in, though he's practically unknown in the United States. Just as well, Connors was once deported for illegal entry into the U.S. when he and a friend hitchhiked to Nashville hoping to meet Hank Snow.

Born in 1936 to a poor, unwed mother, Connors had a rough start in life. He spent time in an orphanage and later a foster home in PEI. Connors said he tried to run away but found it "wasn't easy when you live on an island." He finally left home as a teen and worked odd jobs as he travelled across Canada with his constant companion, a guitar. In 1964, Connors was at a bar in the Maple Leaf Hotel in Timmins, Ontario, when he found himself a nickel short for a beer. The bartender suggested he play a few songs to make up the difference, and that was the start of Connors' singing career. With his trademark black cowboy hat and boots, he stomped his foot to keep rhythm, and the nickname "Stompin' Tom" quickly caught on.

Connors has since won six Junos, honorary degrees, the Order of Canada and had his likeness portrayed on a postage stamp. He was stompin' mad, however, about the federal government's lack of support for Canadian artists and the Americanization of the Canadian music industry. In protest, he sent back his Junos and declined the honour of induction into the Canadian Country Music Hall of Fame. The roadhouse folk hero remains more popular than ever and recently came out of retirement to continue performing his music. Connors, an admitted chain smoker, has said there is only one thing that might make him stop touring—Canada's strict anti-smoking laws, which greatly limit the public places where smokers can light up.

# LITERARY LUNACIES

## Canadian Connection

*It's raining cats and dogs!*
*I wasn't born yesterday.*
*Seeing is believing.*

If any of those sayings ring a bell, you can thank a Canadian for it. His name was Thomas Chandler Haliburton, a witty judge from Windsor, Nova Scotia, with a "quick as a wink" aptitude for penning catchy phrases. In 1836, Haliburton wrote *The Clockmaker: Or, the Sayings and Doings of Sam Slick from Slickville*. Slick was a travelling American salesman who spewed out aphorisms such as "looking for a needle in a haystack," "you can't get blood out of a stone" and "never look a gift horse in the mouth." The book became a bestseller in Canada, the United States and Britain, and was even translated into German. In 1856, Haliburton moved to England, where he died nine years later. He has been called the father of American humour, but back in his native Nova Scotia, the first weekend in August is still celebrated as Sam Slick Day.

### Worst Poet in Canada?

No one knows exactly what happened to James Gay's mental state in the late 1860s. The former innkeeper, carpenter and locksmith from Guelph, Ontario, appears to have suffered from a virus or a brain injury of which he eventually recovered—sort of. Whatever the illness, it left him with a penchant for poetry, and he started to prolifically write poems—a lot of poems, for that matter. He also started talking in rhyme, with phrases such as "nice day, nice day, so says Canada's poet, James Gay." Yes, Gay declared himself "Poet Laureate of Canada and Master of All Poets."

To sell his work, he did what any other savvy marketer might do—he bought a two-headed calf. Gay and his mutant pet travelled to country fairs, where customers paid 10 cents to view his calf and another five cents for a copy of his poems. He even toured Great Britain for a year. When Gay returned to Canada, he learned that his poems hadn't been well received by the media. One newspaper described his poetry as "rot." Gay sued for libel but continued to write and publish. A dedication to Tennyson published in his 1884 book of poems, *Canada's Poet*, included the phrase, "there ought to be no rivalry between us two." Another quote attributed to Gay perhaps best defines his talent—it reads, "Hail our Great Queen in her regalia. One foot in Canada, the other in Australia." Gay passed away in 1891.

### Picky, Picky

*Canadian Idol* winner Nikki Yanofsky sang the Olympic theme song, "I Believe" at the opening ceremonies in February 2010. The song has topped the charts for over 13 weeks, but grammarians protest that its lyrics are less than stellar. The refrain "I believe in the power of you and I" is technically incorrect. The wording should be "I believe in the power of you and me," since "me" is the object of the preposition "of." Tom Cochrane made the same mistake with his song, "Life is a Highway." The Canadian classic rock tune contains the lyrics "a distance between you and I," making grammar teachers and editors wince every time they hear it.

# Secret Writer

When Canadian freelancer Leslie McFarlane saw an advertisement seeking an "Experienced Fiction Writer," he thought it might be a good way to earn a few extra bucks. He got the job and began to write stories from outlines and plots given to him by the Stratemeyer Syndicate of New Jersey. The year was 1926 and McFarlane only received $125 and no royalties, but he didn't mind. McFarlane later moved back to Canada, but he continued to write books under the pen name Franklin W. Dixon. The books, of course, were the *Hardy Boys* mysteries and went on to become the bestselling boys' books in the world until the 1940s. McFarlane, however, had no idea how famous those stories were until much later in his life. He also never revealed that he and Dixon were one and the same person until his autobiography in 1976, just one year before his death.

### The Bard? Or Not the Bard?

Among the portraits thought to be the true representation of William Shakespeare is one that was found tucked upstairs in an Ottawa attic. In 2001, retired engineer Lloyd Sullivan announced that this painting, which had been in his family for generations, may actually be a true likeness of the Bard himself at age 39. On the back was a label with the date 1603 and a claim that this was a painting of "Shakspere," an authentic early spelling of his name. The artist, John Sanders, was known to have briefly associated with Shakespeare's company. Scientific tests on the painting have also indicated that it is from the right time period. So could this be *the* real Shakespeare portrait, a genuine portrayal of the world's most famous writer? Perhaps the other contenders doth protest too much.

## Bye, Bye, Beaver

Maybe it was inevitable. Any magazine with a title that contains a double-entendre slang word for female genitalia was bound to be met with a snicker or two. It wasn't always that way, though. Founded in 1920 by the Hudson's Bay Company, *The Beaver* is one of Canada's oldest and most respectable publications. Its name is synonymous with the fur trade and Canadian history. Now published by Canada's Historical Society, the magazine boasts a print subscription of up to 50,000 copies. But, in this age of Internet filters and cyber-porn, readers complained that they could not access *The Beaver*'s newsletters or emails, not to mention the problem of attracting new readers. "Market research showed us that younger Canadians and women were very, very unlikely to ever buy a magazine called *The Beaver*," explained the magazine's editor-in-chief. "For whatever reason, they are turned off by the name." The magazine officially changed its moniker to *Canada's History* in its April 2010 issue.

## Teeny Tiny Book

Two physicists at Simon Fraser University in British Columbia may need to get their eyes checked. In May 2007, they took the story *Teeny Ted from Turnip Town* by Malcolm Douglas Chaplin and made it into the world's smallest book. It's 30 pages long, but each page is only 0.07 millimetres by 0.10 millimetres, or 20 times smaller than head of a pin. Each letter was made by beams of ions. If you've got $20,000, you can buy one of the 100 copies available. It's definitely a limited edition, and you'll also need to invest in an electron microscope to be able to actually read the words.

# STRANGE MEDICINE

*...what I got by going to Canada was a cold.*

–Henry David Thoreau

*Health Check: Does Canadian medical history tickle your funny bone or scare you to death? Either way, this sampling of stories will be enough to make you scratch your head.*

## Stomach This

In 1822, Alexis St. Martin was accidentally shot, leaving a gaping hole in his stomach. The surgeon, Dr. William Beaumont, thought his patient would surely die, but St. Martin miraculously recovered. However, his stomach wound, a fistula the size of a coin, didn't close. It was the perfect opportunity for Beaumont to learn exactly how the stomach worked. In 1833, he wrote a book entitled *Experiments and Observations on the Gastric Juice and the Physiology of Digestion*. St. Martin eventually outlived Dr. Beaumont but died at the age of 66, poor and an alcoholic. Relatives buried his body in an unmarked grave eight feet underground so it wouldn't be stolen as a curiosity. In 1962, the Canadian Physiological Society erected a plaque near his burial site to honour the man who "through his affliction he served humanity."

### Tastes Bad

You've got to give Frank Buckley credit. This savvy Canadian came up with one of the best (or worst, depending on how you look at it) marketing slogans. Frank's father, William Knapp Buckley, moved to Toronto from Nova Scotia in 1914, where he worked as a pharmacist. During the flu epidemic in 1918, William Buckley invented a cough remedy called Buckley's Mixture, which included herbal ingredients such as pine oil and menthol. He set up the W.K. Buckley Ltd. company in 1920 and, within 20 years, went global with its marketing. When the senior Buckley died in 1978, Frank became president of the company and came up with the slogan, "It tastes awful, and it works!" When asked about the famous concoction, Frank admitted they "can't get rid of the taste. If we do, we will be just another 'me too' cough medicine."

# That's ONE CRAZY CANUCK! The Amazon-Canadian Lady

When Anna Swan was born on August 6, 1846, in Mill Brook, Nova Scotia, her shocked parents couldn't believe the size of their little girl. She tipped the scale at over eight kilograms (18 pounds). Anna was the third of 12 children, and her parents and siblings were all normal sized, but not Anna. By the time she was five years old, she stood over 142 centimetres tall (almost five feet). When she was a teenager, Anna towered over most adult men. Anna quickly outgrew most regular-sized chairs and had to sit on the floor to eat her meals. She likely had a medical condition—excessive growth hormone—that caused her to eventually reach an incredible height of 2.27 metres, or nearly 7 feet 7 inches (that's about a foot higher than your average doorway!).

Intelligent and studious, Anna hoped to become a teacher, but when the famous showman P.T. Barnum heard of her, he successfully convinced the giantess to join his American Museum in 1862. Anna was paid a huge sum of money to act and to give music lessons and lectures to visitors. In 1868, a fire at the museum almost took Anna's life. She was rescued through a hole in the wall and lowered to the ground with a rope held by 18 men. One day, at a circus

☛

social function, Anna met Martin Van Buren Bates, a former Confederate soldier in the Civil War. Martin was a perfect match for Anna. Known as the "Kentucky Giant," he was amazingly slightly *taller* than her. The two fell in love and were married while on tour in London, England, in 1871. Anna wore a special wedding dress and jewellery given to her by Queen Victoria for the occasion.

The next year, Anna gave birth to baby girl, but the unusually large infant was a stillborn. After another tour, the giant couple settled into their Ohio home, a custom-built house with super-high ceilings, where they entertained friends and kept pets, such as their monkey, Buttons. Anna eventually learned she was pregnant again and had another baby, this time a boy. He weighed an astounding 10 kilograms (23 pounds), but sadly, he died shortly after birth. Grief stricken, Anna never had any more children. She led a quiet life until her death from consumption and possibly heart failure in 1888. It was the day before her 42nd birthday.

# And ANOTHER CRAZY ALMOST-CANUCK!

## Dr. Barry's Big Secret

In 1857, Dr. James Miranda Barry was appointed Inspector General of Hospitals for Upper and Lower Canada. The diminutive British physician had a feisty reputation—even Florence Nightingale described him as an arrogant snob. He had a penchant for flamboyant clothes and never travelled far without his manservant, a small pet dog named Psyche, and a goat, for fresh milk to complement his vegetarian diet. Despite his eccentricities, Barry's contributions to Canada were unparalleled. He improved hospital conditions in Montréal, Québec City, Toronto and Kingston. He fought for the poor and sick and, as a chief military physician, encouraged healthier food for recruits as well as special quarters for married soldiers. Unfortunately, Barry developed bronchitis and was forced to return to England.

Before he died in 1865, Barry left specific orders that his clothes not be removed and no autopsy be performed on his body. A servant woman named Sophia Bishop, however, didn't get the instructions and experienced the shock of her life as she was preparing Barry's body for burial. According to Bishop, Barry was actually a *woman* and had stretch marks on "her" abdomen, meaning she may have once been pregnant. No autopsy was performed, but a staff surgeon later admitted that he personally thought Barry may have been a hermaphrodite. Evidence later surfaced that Barry was born Margaret Bulkeley and, disguised as a boy, graduated as a doctor in Scotland and joined the British Army, where at the time no physical examination was required. Barry worked in South Africa and the Caribbean and even performed the first successful Cesarean section by a British doctor. Since "he" was really most likely a "she," then Barry was also the first female doctor in North America but preferred to take that secret to her, er, "his" grave.

# DEADLY DISEASES

## Canadian Lepers

For most of human history, just the word "leprosy" was enough to send chills down one's spine. Although presently treatable, this hideous disease disfigures the body to the point where fingers, noses and toes fall off, and it is still prevalent in many poorer areas of the world. It's also part of a strange and appalling chapter in Canadian history. In April 1844, New Brunswick passed a law called "An Act to Prevent the Spread of a Disorder now Existing in Certain Parts of the Counties of Gloucester and Northumberland." That summer, 18 lepers, aged eight through 46 years old, were sent to live in isolation on Sheldrake Island. Five years later, the lepers were moved to a lazaretto, or leper hospital, in Tracadie, New Brunswick. Tracadie took in lepers from across Canada, except for those who were Chinese. Chinese lepers had been banished to D'Arcy Island, off Vancouver Island, since the early 1890s. Every few months, a supply ship would arrive with food for the living and coffins for the dead. Eventually, medical officials denounced the ill treatment of Chinese lepers. In one case, two men almost died when they were shipped from New York to D'Arcy Island—as it turned out, one of the men didn't even have the dreaded disorder. The ill-treatment of lepers continued until the development of new drugs that helped prevent the disease. In 1965, the last of the Canadian lazarettos was permanently closed.

## Mosquito Revenge

**Question:**  *What insects love math?*
**Answer:**  *Mosquitoes, because they divide your attention, multiply quickly, subtract from pleasure and add to misery.*

The mosquitoes in Upsala, Ontario, are so big that they can carry off a full-size man. Thankfully, the "man" in question isn't

real and neither is the five-metre-long fibreglass mosquito statue, ready for dinner with a knife and fork. The Manitoban town of Komarno, which means "mosquito" in Ukrainian, also built an equally giant stinger sculpture in 1984. Known as the "Mosquito Capital of Canada," Komarno is situated just north of Winnipeg, another bug-plagued city. Winnipeggers often resort to using fogging trucks to spray insecticides on the pesky bloodsuckers. Aside from being a nuisance, mosquitoes can carry diseases, including the West Nile Virus, which was unheard of in North America before 2004. And if you think Canada is immune to malaria, the most widely known mosquito-born disease, be glad you weren't working along the Rideau and Cataraqui rivers in Ontario during the early 19th century. Back then, malaria was called "ague" and was thought to be caused by bad air (as in *mal*, the French word for "bad," and *aire*). The wetlands and swampy bogs of the area were potent breeding grounds for mosquitoes during the warm summer months. Between 1826 and 1832, count-less workers building the Rideau Canal succumbed to malaria.

# Scary Workplace

Winnipeg, Manitoba, is home to one of the world's most secure germ laboratories. Good thing too, because sections of the Canadian Science Centre for Human and Animal Health contain some of the most lethal viruses in the world. We're talking Ebola, Lassa, HIV and other nasty stuff. In 2000, the Centre was completed after 10 years at a cost of $172 million. Its laboratories have four levels of containment, from the "high-school-biology-class-like" Level 1 to the "it'll-never-get-out-of-here" Level 4. The Level-4 lab is essentially a concrete box that took a full two years to build. The walls are covered with 30 coats of special paint and an epoxy layer almost eight centimetres thick.

## SARS Fears

In late 2002, a new, deadly virus emerged in southern China. By the following March, a 64-year-old doctor staying at a hotel in Hong Kong unknowingly spread it to other hotel guests, including a 78-year-old Canadian woman. She took a plane back to Toronto where she developed the SARS symptoms: fever, aches, dry cough and a shortness of breath. When the woman, her son and another elderly man in the same hospital died, doctors realized that this virus was different and identified it as Severe Acute Respiratory Syndrome, or the SARS coronavirus.

By March 26, Ontario announced a public health emergency. Hospital staff donned masks, gloves and goggles. Anyone who may have had contact with SARS victims—and that included thousands of people—was quarantined. Public events were cancelled and, worst of all, the World Health Organization declared Toronto a high-risk destination and issued a global travel warning. Tourism in the city ground to a halt, with estimated losses to Canadian businesses at over $1 billion. Over the next few months, Toronto suffered two waves of SARS outbreaks, in which 44 Canadians from the Toronto area, including two nurses, died from the disease. By July, SARS was under control, but the city was still reeling. To help out, a "Toronto Rocks" concert was held in Downsview Park, with bands such as AC/DC, The Guess Who, Rush and The Rolling Stones taking part. Over a million people attended what was later called SARStock or SARSapalooza, making it the biggest single-day concert ever held in North America.

## Swine Flu Mania

In 2009, the "Swine Flu" hit North America, and the media went crazy. According to them, this was the pandemic everyone had been anticipating, and it was going to be deadly. Travel warnings to Mexico, where the disease had first struck, were issued, and thousands of Canadians cancelled their vacations. When two young people in Ontario suddenly died from the disease, health officials hammered home the message: Canadians *needed* to get the H1N1 vaccine as soon as it was available to prevent an outbreak.

When the day came for Canadians to get their shots, it was complete mayhem. Ontarians had up to wait up to six hours in line, and this was only for the elderly, the very young and other persons considered "at risk." Overwhelmed with the crowds, some clinics closed early. At one point, Calgary, a city with a population of over a million people, had only *four* clinics open. When word got out that healthy team members of the Calgary Flames had jumped the queue and had received their shots early, people were furious. Fortunately, the widespread Swine Flu pandemic never materialized. Panic subsided, and life went back to normal…at least for now.

The term "H1N1" strangely and suddenly replaced the "Swine Flu" during the height of the media's frenzy because of protests from the pork industry. Even though the disease could not be caught by eating cooked pork, the name alone was enough to put a serious dent in the bacon business.

# HUMAN POPSICLES

## Frozen Stiff

It was a frigid February night in 1994 when two-year-old Karlee Kosolofski stepped outside her home in Rouleau, Saskatchewan, wearing only thin nightclothes. Her mother was fast asleep, unaware that Karlee had tried to follow her father out as he left for shift work at 2:00 AM. Trapped in the –22°C temperature, Karlee quickly succumbed to the extreme cold. She was found six hours later, her tiny body almost frozen solid. Hospital workers determined that her core temperature was a mere 14.2°C—a normal reading was 37°C. Slowly, they warmed her back up with a heart-and-lung machine. Amazingly, Karlee recovered. Her severely frostbitten left leg had to be amputated and she did require skin grafts, but she did not suffer any brain damage. Experts believe her small size and young age were factors in her survival.

She was one of the few human beings who have ever been successfully "unfrozen." A similar event occurred on February 24, 2001, when 13-month-old Erika Nordby also wandered outside in the middle of the night. When she was discovered at 3:00 AM, the temperature outside was –20°C. Clinically dead and with no measurable heartbeat, Erika's body temperature of 16°C was slowly brought back up to normal. Except for a few skin grafts, Erika made a full recovery and went home after five weeks. By sheer coincidence, one of the paramedics who had been on the scene when Erika was found also assisted with Karlee's rescue.

### Buried and Barely Alive

Her husband called it a "Christmas miracle." His 55-year-old wife, Donna Molnar, had gone missing three days earlier during blizzard conditions. Molnar's abandoned SUV was soon found in the countryside near Ancaster, Ontario, but there were no signs of Molnar. Thanks to a search-and-rescue dog, she was finally found, frostbitten and suffering from hypothermia but very much alive. Molnar had been buried in 60 centimetres of snow with only her face exposed. Experts say she was extremely lucky, as the snow likely insulated her from the sub-zero temperatures and kept her alive long enough to be rescued.

# SIX FEET UNDER

*They say there are only two certainties in life: death and taxes. While the taxes in Canada may be enough to give you a heart attack, sooner or later the grim reaper visits everyone. We Canadians have had our fair share of peculiar stories about that inevitable one-way trip we'll all face one day. Some of these might even make you glad you're still alive and kicking!*

## Buried Again and Again and Again

Poor General Isaac Brock—October 13 was not a good day for him. It was bad enough that the War of 1812 hero was fatally shot on that date in 1812 (his aide-de-camp, John MacDonnell, was also killed). For the next three days, Brock lay in state at Government House before being buried at nearby Fort George. You'd think that he could then rest in peace in the sweet hereafter, but no, it was not to be. The Upper Canada legislature wanted to make a monument to him several kilometres away, but it took over a decade to raise enough funds. Finally, in 1824, on the anniversary of his death, October 13, Brock was reburied. Over 5000 spectators came to see the war hero reinterred in a vault at the base of the monument. Eternal life for Brock was again peaceful until April 17, 1840, when a disturbed rebel, still angry at the British, set off an explosion that damaged the monument's tower. Officials made plans for a new tower, but construction didn't actually start for years. By then, it was necessary for the remains of Brock and MacDonnell to be moved to temporary graves until the fourth, and final, burial took place on October 13, 1853. This time, 15,000 people came to see Brock get buried again. Finishing touches on the tower were finally completed in 1856, and it was officially opened on, you guessed it, October 13, 1859.

William Lyon Mackenzie tried to hide a copy of his controversial newspaper, the *Colonial Advocate*, inside a block on the Brock monument. When the lieutenant-governor discovered Mackenzie's sneaky stunt, the paper was ordered removed.

## Take a Stand, Forever

Louis Riel's commander-in-chief and fellow Métis, Gabriel Dumont, was buried standing up in Batoche cemetery near the Saskatchewan River. Some say he wanted to see the enemy approaching from the other side of the river, while others think it was because he just wanted a nice view of the hereafter.

# Dig 'Em Up

Good bodies were hard to come by during the middle of the 19th century. Because legally available cadavers were in such short supply, medical students in Montréal secretly dug up bodies from cemeteries for dissection practice. In return for a bribe, cemetery workers marked the freshly made graves so the medical students could pop by in the middle of the night and disinter the bodies. One account describes how they removed the corpses' clothing, wrapped the bodies in blankets and even tobogganed them down the Côte des Neiges hill. The nefarious practice ended when the 1884 "Act to Regulate and Facilitate the Study of Anatomy" made it easier to obtain deceased human bodies for medical studies.

## A Winnipeg Mummy

No one complains if you keep paying the bills. Such was the case with retired municipal worker, Jim Sulker. The 53-year-old Winnipegger went to bed one night and never woke up. Similar deaths aren't unusual; people die in their sleep all the time. But when Sulker's time on Earth came to an end sometime in November 2002, no one discovered it for almost two years. How could such a thing happen? As a multiple sclerosis sufferer, Sulker had been on a disability pension, and all his bill payments were on automatic withdrawal. As a reclusive man who was not particularly close to his family, no one suspected anything was wrong when they didn't hear from Sulker. When visitors came to his tidy, upscale condominium and knocked on his door sometime in 2003, no one answered, so they simply assumed he wasn't at home—perhaps he had gone on an extended vacation.

It wasn't until August 2004, some 20 months after his death, that Sulker's father asked police to check in on his son. His mummified remains were found exactly where he had expired. A newspaper dated November 21, 2002, and an out-of-date calendar helped to narrow down his approximate date of death, and an autopsy determined that Sulker likely died of natural causes. The warm, dry air in his residence contributed to Sulker's mummification and the total lack of any typical bodily decomposition smell. Nothing in Sulker's home rotted away, except maybe the food in his refrigerator.

# A Grave Inscription

Rushes old pioneer cemetery in southern Ontario contains one of the more unusual messages on a grave marker. Samuel Bean was born in 1842 and grew up to become a medical doctor and evangelist minister (some say he read the entire Bible over 65 times). Bean married Henrietta Furry, but she died after only seven months of wedded bliss. He later married Susanna Clegg, but she too passed away shortly after their marriage. The townsfolk didn't have time to question the deaths, however, because they were too busy trying to decipher the cryptogram Bean had engraved on the two women's grave marker. The original stone eventually became too weathered to read, but in 1982 the local heritage society erected a copy next to it. The inscription consisted of a seemingly random jumble of 225 letters and numbers. If read from the middle in a zig-zag counterclockwise direction, the memorial's words finally appear:

### *The Bean Cryptogram:*

*In memoriam Henrietta, 1st wife of S. Bean M.D. who died 27th Sep 1865 aged 23 years 2 months and 17 days & Susanna his second wife who died 27 April 1867 aged 26 years 3 months and 15 days. 2 better wives 1 man never had. They were gifts from God and are now in Heaven. May God help me S.B. to meet them there.*

### The Oven Door Face

The mansion at 31 Leinster Street, Saint John, New Brunswick, may have been demolished in 1987, but a curious artifact discovered in its foundations still remains. The house was turned into a restaurant in the late 1970s, and one day a patron interested in architecture came to check out the cellar. In it, she found an old brick oven and opened its iron door only to come face to face with the startling image of a young girl with bangs and short hair. She took a Polaroid photograph and showed the owner. He tried to scrub the door with scouring pads, but the image just wouldn't disappear. Museum experts later concluded that it wasn't a oven but rather a makeshift crematorium. The original owner of the building had a young daughter who died, likely during a cholera epidemic, and was probably cremated. The intense fire created enough light and carbons to "etch" her image right onto the oven door forever.

# Cariboo Cameron

John Angus "Cariboo" Cameron grew up in eastern Ontario and made his money during the gold rushes of California and British Columbia in the 1850s. Wealthy and ready to find a wife, he travelled to Ontario in 1860 and soon married 28-year-old Margaret Sophia. Cameron was 40 at the time but hoped to settle into a comfortable life with his beloved "Sophia." When he learned of gold out in the Cariboo, near Barkerville, British Columbia, Cameron once again got the itch. He wanted to head out west, but Sophia was reluctant to leave her hometown. She finally agreed, and the couple and their four-month-old baby, Alice, set out on the arduous cross-Canada trek. Sadly, by the time they reached Victoria, their baby had become sick and died. Sophia sorely missed her home back in Ontario, but the couple, along with other miners, trudged onward.

In the fall of 1862, tragedy struck again. Sophia gave birth to a stillborn baby and subsequently developed typhoid fever.

Her dying wish was that her husband would take her body away from what she called "this awful place." The faithful husband agreed, and when Sophia died on October 23, Cameron temporarily buried her until he could finance the return voyage home. That winter, Cameron hired a few men to help him out. They pulled Sophia's coffin on a toboggan, and when the men quit, Cameron bought horses. The horses eventually died of exhaustion, but by now Cameron had reached the Fraser River. Sophia, preserved in alcohol within her tin coffin, was then loaded on a steamship to be taken to Victoria. Once there, Cameron was forced to place her in a temporary tomb as he needed to return to the Cariboo to work his claim and mine for more gold. When he was finished, he dug Sophia back up and embarked upon the long voyage down the west coast through the Panama Canal and onto New York.

Cameron faced yet another roadblock in New York. Customs officials, suspicious of the coffin's contents, wanted to open it, but Cameron refused. As a compromise, he paid a New York customs worker to accompany him back to Ontario and witness Sophia's final burial. At long last, Sophia's dying wish had been granted, and Cameron remained in the area. He remarried three years after Sophia's death, but gossip and rumours still plagued him. Was Sophia still alive? Had Cameron murdered her and smuggled gold over in the coffin? By 1873, a fed-up Cameron made an announcement that her coffin would once again be exhumed; he wanted to prove once and for all that, yes, her corpse was in there. Hundreds of spectators gathered for the event. The tin coffin was cut open and there, inside the box, lay the very well-preserved Sophia. Cameron reburied her in a different cemetery and later moved with his second wife back to British Columbia. He died in 1888 and was buried in the now-ghost town of Cameronton.

# That's ONE CRAZY CANUCK!

## The Great Stork Race

When Torontonian Charles Vance Millar died in 1926, he left a strange will. The wealthy corporate lawyer didn't have any dependants or likeable relatives, so he chose to distribute his money in a very unorthodox fashion. He left one share of stock in the Kenilworth Jockey Club Racetrack to a number of Christian ministers (all avidly against gambling). He also left a share of the O'Keefe Brewing Company stock to each Protestant Lodge in Toronto and their respective ministers (who were against drinking). He bestowed a home in Jamaica to three of his lawyer friends who didn't like each other at all, and finally, he offered a huge sum of money to the Toronto woman who had the most children within 10 years of his death. Government officials tried to contest this last amendment in Millar's will, but women's groups protested and pointed a finger at the clergy who had unscrupulously claimed their prizes.

By 1936, the Great Stork Race was over, and several women stepped forward to claim the money. Two contestants were subsequently disqualified: one had given birth to 10 children but only five by her actual husband, while another woman had nine but half had been stillborn and she couldn't present the birth certificates. In the end, four women, each with nine children, were declared winners. Each woman received $165,000 and instructions on how to use birth control.

# MURDER MOST FOUL

## Graveyard of the St. Lawrence

Over 400 ships have been wrecked near Anticosti Island at the mouth of the St. Lawrence. One was the timber ship, *Granicus,* that hit a reef in November 1828. The crew and passengers were able to make it to shore and likely wintered at one of the island's abandoned camps. The following spring, a whaling schooner came across the survivors' camp and made a horrific discovery. They found seven severed heads, a bushel full of bones, body parts and the clothing from the passengers, which had included two women and three children. The victims had all been murdered, then eaten. The shocked whalers also discovered a large, recently deceased man lying in a hammock, whom they deduced was the well-fed murderer.

### He Blew Up a Plane to Kill His Wife

Albert Guay wanted out of his marriage. Divorce was difficult to obtain in Québec during the 1940s, so he had to find another way. The jeweller bought a plane ticket for his 29-year-old wife, Rita, and convinced her to pick up a few items for his business. At 10:45 AM on September 9, 1949, the DC-3 en route from Montréal to Baie Comeau near Sault-au-Cochon, Québec, suddenly exploded. No one, including Rita and the 22 other passengers onboard, survived.

At first, officials were puzzled as to what could have happened—exploding passenger planes were virtually unheard of. Shortly after the crash, Marguerite Reust-Pitre, a woman who had been seen expediting a parcel onto the plane, broke down and confessed that her secret lover, Albert Guay, had asked her brother to make a bomb. The bomb was supposed to go off while the plane was flying over the St. Lawrence, where all the evidence would have been lost forever in the deep waters, but the plane, being five minutes late, had exploded over land instead. Guay was hanged in 1951, as was Marguerite's bomb-making brother the following year. Marguerite herself went to the gallows in 1953, the last woman ever to be hanged in Canada.

## The Sleepwalker Murders

Technically, you can only be found guilty of a crime if you were conscious at the time it occurred. But how can an unconscious person actually commit a crime? The answer is if he or she is sleepwalking. There have been around 70 legal cases worldwide involving "homicidal somnambulism," or the act of killing someone while sleepwalking. One such event occurred just outside Toronto after a 23-year-old father fell asleep while watching television. He later walked into a police station with blood on his clothes and said, "I think I killed someone." Indeed, the man had driven 20 kilometres in the night, walked into his in-laws' home and attacked them while they were sleeping. The defence argued that the accused had experienced severe stress over a gambling addiction which, combined with a history of sleepwalking, made him totally unconscious at the time of the murders. A jury, and later a Supreme Court decision, agreed, and he was acquitted of murdering his mother-in-law and attempted murder on his father-in-law.

Billed as "An Arresting Experience," the Police Centennial Museum in east Vancouver isn't your ordinary art gallery. Among its collection are police artifacts, historical documents, a firearms collection and a makeshift morgue with "items" taken from, ahem, actual autopsies.

### Jack the Ripper, a Canadian?
Just before he was hanged in Chicago for murdering a man by using strychnine, Dr. Thomas Neil Cream said, "I am Jack the..."

The hangman's noose prevented Cream from finishing his sentence, but could it be that the medical graduate of McGill University and former Ontario resident was actually Jack the Ripper? No one knows for sure, but there is a distinct possibility. For one, Cream had a history of violence against women, but he usually escaped conviction. Secondly, he was familiar with England, having previously travelled there. Lastly, his handwriting closely resembled the script on Jack the Ripper's letters. Cream was egotistical, and it wouldn't have been beyond him to brag of his actions. Although he was supposedly in prison in 1888, the time when Jack the Ripper's killing spree took place, the prison system was extremely corrupt, and it is conceivable Cream bribed his way to freedom and returned to London. Until Jack the Ripper's identity is confirmed, this Canadian doctor is definitely a suspect.

# FALLING DOWN THE FALLS

## Where Is PETA When You Need Them?

Perhaps the strangest stunt to ever occur at Niagara Falls was put on by the Edge Hotel in September 1827. In a crazy bid to attract tourists, they loaded two bears, a raccoon, a buffalo, a dog and a few birds in an old schooner and sent it over the Falls. Only one goose survived, although it's not known if the poor bird later ended up on a dinner plate.

### Those Who Died...

*July 11, 1920:* Charles Stephens from Bristol, England, went over the Falls in a barrel with a weight tied to his feet. After the plunge, pieces of the broken barrel were recovered with one of

Stephen's arms still strapped to the wood. It was the arm with the tattoo inscription, "Forget Me Not Annie."

*July 5, 1930:* George Stathakis, a Greek chef from Buffalo, plunged over the Falls in a barrel, this time with his pet turtle named Sonny. Only Sonny came out alive.

*August 5, 1951:* Thousands of spectators watched William "Red" Hill Jr. challenge the Falls in his contraption of fishnets, inner tubes and paraphernalia called "The Thing." Whatever it was, it didn't work.

*June 5, 1990:* Jesse W. Sharp, sans helmet or lifejacket because he wanted his friends to be able to videotape his stunt, climbed into his plastic kayak and went over the Falls. His body was never recovered.

*October 1, 1995:* A Californian by the name of Robert Overacker decided to bring attention to homelessness by taking his rocket-propelled Jet-Ski over the Falls, then parachuting off it. Unfortunately, his parachute either didn't deploy or fell away, and he rode the Jet-Ski to the bottom. Overacker's body was found by the *Maid of the Mist* tourist boat the next day.

# And Three Who Survived...

*July 9, 1960:* With only a life vest for protection, nine-year-old Roger Woodward accidentally went over the Falls when he and Deanne, his teenaged sister, along with Jim Honeycutt, a family friend, all fell out of Honeycutt's boat on the upper Niagara River. Woodward's sister was rescued at the brink, but Roger and Honeycutt were swept over the Falls. Roger sustained only minor cuts and bruises, but Honeycutt perished in the tragedy—his body was recovered four days later.

*July 3, 1984:* Karel Soucek of Hamilton, Ontario, survived the Falls after he went over the edge in a barrel. Soucek died the following year at the Houston Astrodome while trying to recreate the stunt in a water tank.

*October 20, 2003:* Kirk Jones of Michigan became the first person ever to survive the Falls completely unaided. Jones jumped into the Niagara River with only the clothes on his back. Sources say he was either depressed or simply very drunk.

### Taking the Plunge
Oscar Wilde once called Niagara Falls the "second major disappointment of American married life," but to daredevils, it's the ultimate thrill.

# Missed Out: A Houdini in Niagara Stunt

It was a Canadian who might have delivered the fatal blow to famous escape artist Harry Houdini. On October 22, 1926, several McGill University students visited Houdini in his dressing room at the Princess Theatre in Montréal. Houdini had always been proud of his strong stomach muscles and often let men punch him in the gut to demonstrate his toughness. The students asked if his boasts were true. Houdini couldn't resist taking up the challenge, but before he could prepare himself, one of the students hit Houdini squarely in the abdomen. Despite the pain, Houdini was unaware his appendix had ruptured and continued as if nothing was wrong. Infection eventually set in, and Houdini passed away several days later on October 31—Halloween. Interestingly, Houdini may have been seriously considering an escape trick featuring the Niagara Falls before his untimely death. He wrote in his notebook that he was mulling over the idea of sealing himself in a crate, which would then go over the Falls. Unfortunately, Niagara's most exciting escape never came to pass.

# HANGIN' IN

## A History of Hanging Shows

The first recorded execution in Canada took place in 1542, when a man was put to death for theft. In 1763, Marie-Joseph Corriveau was hanged for axing her second husband to death. Her body was then left to decompose for one month in an iron cage displayed in public. Apparently, her imprisoned spirit haunted passersby for months until the cage was finally buried. It was rediscovered over 80 years later and sold to a museum in the U.S. but has since disappeared. In February 1869, Patrick Whelan was publicly hanged for shooting Member of Parliament D'Arcy McGee in Ottawa. His was thought to be the last public hanging in Canada, but later that year, a man named Nicholas Melady was sent to the gallows for murder. He was put to death in front of a small crowd, but thousands of latecomers were disappointed when they discovered that they had missed one of the last public hangings in Canada.

## Hanging Problems

It happens—things don't always go as planned. Public executions, some of which occurred in Canada before the death penalty was repealed, are no exception. Poor George Dowie was one such unfortunate soul. Dowie, a sailor, stabbed a man to death in Charlottetown, PEI, during a drunken brawl and was sentenced to hang on April 6, 1869. Over 1500 people came to watch the spectacle. His last words comprised an eight-page treatise, so Dowie recited them sitting down. Half an hour later, he was ready to die. The noose went around his neck and the trap door flung open, but the rope accidentally broke. Dowie woke up back in jail, confused, but was assured the noose would soon be fixed. True to their word, the execution resumed one hour later. The shaken Dowie needed to be carried up to the scaffold and everything seemed to be going well—until he hit the ground. The new noose had been strung too long. After this final technical glitch, the semi-conscious Dowie was lifted up for one more try. He was pronounced dead 15 minutes later, but the entire incident cast a pall over the question of capital punishment.

# The Death Mask of Woodstock

In the southwestern Ontario town of Woodstock, you'll find a historic yellow brick building that now houses a public health unit. Built in the mid-1800s, this was the former courthouse and jail for the region. It was scheduled for demolition in 1977, but local heritage groups rallied to save it. One reason for its importance was a unique carving on its archway that had

a macabre history. Look closely at the right side of the arch at the entrance, and you'll see a face with a sad, almost pained expression sculpted. It's the face of a man named Thomas Cook, who was hanged there in 1862 for beating his wife to death. Unfortunately, the executioner had made Cook's rope too long, and he was gruesomely decapitated. His head was even said to have rolled out toward the crowd. To ensure that such a spectacle never happened again—or maybe to remind potential criminals that it might—officials agreed to memorialize Cook's face on the building.

## Call the Professional

In 1912, one criminal took almost 20 minutes to die of strangulation after his execution went awry. Following the incident, the Canadian government quietly asked a professional, Arthur English, if he could take over as official executioner. English, who used the name "Arthur Ellis" in his work life, took the job and moved to Montréal. Throughout his "distinguished" career, he performed over 600 executions. As executioner, one of his tasks was to ensure the hanging rope was the correct length for the condemned. If the rope was too short, the felon would simply hang there until he or she strangled to death; too long and it could literally pull the head right off the shoulders. One of his, er, "clients" was Thomasina Sarao. Ellis didn't adjust for her actual weight, and the process accidentally decapitated her. He was also the executioner of Ronald Turpin and Arthur Lucas. When told that they might be the last two people to be hanged in Canada, Turpin replied, "Some consolation!" Ellis' last year of work wasn't a good one—Lucas' execution didn't go as planned, and he was almost decapitated; there was blood everywhere. Capital punishment was abolished in 1976, but Ellis continued to receive a $200 per month stipend until 1985, a decision by the sheriff of York County just in case the politicians decided to bring the death penalty back again.

 If Ellis's name sounds familiar, it's because the Crime Writers of Canada named its annual literary crime awards after him: the Arthur Ellis Awards. The award is, of course, a wooden, hand-carved "hanged man" figurine with a noose around its neck. "I'd like to thank the Academy, and the jury!"

# Help Wanted

In 1778, on Prince Edward Island, Elizabeth Mukely stole seven pounds from her employer. Since the British colony still followed British law, she was sentenced to death. But who would hang a woman? No one could be found. The sheriff even placed "hangman wanted ads" in the local paper, but no one wanted the job. After months of waiting and then hoping that maybe someone new arriving on a ship from Europe would take the job, still no one did. Elizabeth was therefore simply banished from the colony but left very much alive.

# ALIENS ARE MOST WELCOME

*Strange knows no boundaries when it comes to Canada. I'm talking out-of-this-world places found right here at home, as well as cringe-worthy supernatural events that have taken place on Canadian soil and in our skies. Many have been well documented, but try to get an explanation from our government and, well, you're out of luck. Unless, that is, they find out it's good for tourism…*

## UFO Landing Strip

The town of St. Paul, Alberta, wanted to do something different, off the wall and perhaps a little bit outrageous—something that would put the community on the map and maybe bring in a few more tourists. Half-jokingly, it was suggested that they build a UFO landing pad—it could be a goodwill gesture toward any extraterrestrials that wanted to land peacefully. Why not? Flying saucers were a hot topic in the '60s, and what better way to attract media attention?

And so, St. Paul became the site of the world's first UFO landing pad. At a cost of approximately $11,000—not much when you consider how much regular terrestrial landing strips cost—the famous structure was ceremoniously opened in 1967 with the help of Minister of Defence Paul Hellyer, who was flown in by helicopter. The 12-metre-wide pad had a sign that declared:

> *Republic of St. Paul (Stargate Alpha). The area under the World's First UFO Landing Pad was designated international by the Town of St. Paul as a symbol of our faith that mankind will maintain the outer universe free from national wars and strife. That future travel in space will be safe for all intergalactic beings, all visitors from earth or otherwise are welcome to this territory and to the Town of St. Paul.*

Years later, Hellyer retired and became an outspoken supporter for governments to disclose any secret documentation of extraterrestrial contact. He should know because he worked with Canadian and American officials at the highest levels—but I digress. Back in the '60s, everyone was ready for any sort of alien invasion, preferably the friendly kind. Unfortunately, after the initial publicity, the landing pad didn't attract any aliens or very many tourists, for that matter. In 1982, it finally received a much needed new coat of paint just before a visit from Mother Teresa. Fittingly, the saintly nun declared, while standing on the landing pad, that "If there is sickness in outer space, we would go there too."

Interest in the pad grew during the mid-1990s, and a UFO museum was even built near it. Here, visitors could read recent reports of UFOs, abductions and various unexplained phenomenon taken from a 1-800-UFO hotline set up in 1995 and staffed by volunteers. In 1998, a UFO conference was held that attracted 500 registrants from as far away as Las Vegas. St. Paul had made its mark. It had become what it strived to be, a welcoming town to earthlings and extraterrestrials alike.

## Live Long and Prosper…in Vulcan, Alberta

Not to be outdone, Vulcan, Alberta, has its own special other-worldly connection. The town, about 130 kilometres southeast of Calgary, was named after the blacksmith of the Roman gods in the early 1900s. That all changed in the '60s and '70s when the word "Vulcan" became synonymous with the hit television series and movie franchise, *Star Trek*, as the home planet of one of the main characters, Spock. In 1995, a welder named Gary McKinnon was commissioned to build an 8.5-metre-long *Enterprise*-like "ship" in the hopes that tourists from around the world would come to pay homage to it. Three years later, a 16-metre-tall space station (tourism centre) was added. A plaque that greeted visitors in English, Vulcan and Klingon was also mounted, and before long, throngs of *Star Trek* fans made the prairie trek to Vulcan. Many came to attend the annual VulCON Spock Days-Galaxyfest weekend.

The real Vulcans (the residents of the town, that is) were quite happy with all the publicity they were getting until the latest reboot, *Star Trek XI,* came out in May 2009. It was billed to "go where no *Star Trek* film had gone before," but unfortunately, that didn't include Vulcan, Alberta. Hollywood brass committed a huge oversight and left the town out in the cold; they couldn't even get a screening of the movie! So what if they didn't have a "movie theatre," per se; everyone was prepared to watch it in a gymnasium. Residents tried not show any emotion over the illogical snub, but they eventually went to the media. Even Leonard Nimoy, the actor who played the original Spock, got into the act and went to bat for the small Alberta town. "The people of Vulcan deserve their day in the sun," he told the Canadian press.

Eventually, a lottery was held for 300 lucky winners to be beamed to a special screening at the nearest theatre, an hour away in Calgary. The town's mission was deemed a success. Nimoy even promised to make a special visit to Vulcan, which he fulfilled on April 23, 2010. After all this hoopla, Vulcan, Alberta, is now officially the "Star Trek Capital of Canada."

# AND WHAT PLANET ARE YOU FROM, EH?

## I'm a Martian

In the late 1990s, René Joly filed a lawsuit against Canada's defence minister, Art Eggleton, and various companies, claiming they were trying to kill him because he was a Martian. Joly said he was cloned from debris NASA took from Mars in the 1960s and represented himself during the case. In 1999, a judge found Joly "polite, articulate and intelligent" but ruled that because Joly was not human, he could not be heard in a court of Earthlings.

### Those Odd Raelians

The Raelians are one strange cult who believe we all descended from extraterrestrials. Their founder, Claude Vorilhon, is a former part-time journalist and race-car driver from France. He claims he saw a UFO on December 13, 1973, and an ET from the craft instructed him to adopt the name Rael and to bring a message to humanity. Over the next 30 years, Vorilhon and his Raelians established their headquarters near Valcourt, Québec. They even built a UFO theme park, complete with a spaceship replica and giant human DNA molecule, but decided to sell the properties in 2007 so they could relocate to the U.S., where people might be more understanding.

## Weird Windigo

Kenora, in northern Ontario, is known as the "Windigo Capital of the World," which isn't such a great designation when you consider that a Windigo is a cannibalistic spirit from First Nations lore that can possess humans and cause them to snack on other humans. The Windigo stories go way back, and one account from 1799 describes a hunter who ate his own sister.

# That's ONE CRAZY CANUCK! Brother Twelve

Perhaps it was his strict religious upbringing, or maybe he was just plain crazy, but Edward Wilson went on to become one of British Columbia's most infamous con men. Also known as Amiel de Valdes or Swami Siva, Wilson was a guru, self-proclaimed psychic, occult figure and cult leader. He travelled the world, visiting Egypt and China, and picked up tips on how to be a spiritualist and a fortune teller. During a séance, he declared that 11 supernatural masters had made him number 12. Now dubbed, fittingly, "Brother Twelve," his mission was to start a community in Nanaimo, on Vancouver Island. The "Aquarian Foundation" began in 1927 and was even registered by the Societies Act of British Columbia. Members of Wilson's group gave up all their worldly possessions, especially money. With loads of cash floating around, Wilson even convinced former U.S. Treasury agent Robert England to join the foundation and manage the finances.

Wilson was a good con man—so good that he once rendezvoused with a potential recruit, a rich American woman named Mabel Boyd, at a Toronto hotel and successfully duped her. He knew that she liked animals, so he prepared by training some pigeons to land on him on cue. When Mabel arrived, he took her to the park and said the Eleven Masters would speak to him and send him a bird with their message. Sure enough, the pigeons landed on him, looking for seed in his ear. He said the Masters where speaking to him through the bird and were asking for money. Astonished, Mabel handed over a few hefty cheques—after all, she thought Wilson was, according to visions she had been having, the Egyptian god Osiris reincarnated.

With his goatee, Wilson had that true guru look—women often fell victim to his hypnotic ways. One was a Mrs. Mrytle Baumgartner, who left her husband and children for him when he convinced her she was the reincarnation of his mate, Isis. Another was Mrs. Mary Connally, a wealthy but elderly widow—Wilson used her money to buy nearby Valdes Island. Yet Wilson's most fearless female companion was his mistress Mabel Skottowe, also known as Madame Zee. She literally cracked a bullwhip to keep everyone in line.

Eventually, members of the foundation dwindled from an initial 100 or so to a scant dozen followers. Pretty soon, they too were sick and tired of scary Brother Twelve and Madame Zee. Lawsuits were filed and disgruntled followers went to the police, only to return and find the two had left the island. Before they disappeared, though, Brother Twelve and Madame Zee trashed the place. In the end, the courts gave Valdes Island back to Mary Connally. No one is exactly sure what happened to Brother Twelve or where he died, or if he faked his death. His real-life brother later wrote a book about him and claimed he died in Australia, while others say he died in Switzerland while pretending to be Madame Zee's first husband.

## No Witches Allowed

Witches of Canada, you have been warned. In 2009, a Toronto woman was charged under the Criminal Code for posing as a witch. According to the police, the woman allegedly befriended a Toronto area lawyer and convinced him she had business contacts who could help him become more profitable. The woman claimed to be from a long line of witches and gave him a tarot card reading. During it, she said the spirit of his deceased sister could guide him to financial success and urged him to spend more money to access this information. No word yet if a hex was placed on any judge or other justice official involved in the case.

Daniel Vuil, a Protestant miller, was executed for witchcraft in Québec in October 1662. Apparently, he tormented a servant girl with demons when she refused to marry him. A subsequent exorcism by Bishop Laval also didn't work.

## The Nostradamus Prophecy of Montréal

The famous French prophet, Nostradamus, wrote a quatrain in his *Centuries* collection of 1555 that may or may not make reference to Montréal. Verse VII, 32, also known as the "Canadian prophecy," reads as follows:

> *Du Mont Royal naistre d'une casane*
> *Qui duc, & compte viendra tyranniser*
> *Dresser copie de la marche Millane,*
> *Favence, Florence d'or & gens espusier.*

> *(From the bank of Montereale will be born one*
> *who bores and calculates becoming a tyrant.*
> *To raise a force in the marches of Milan,*
> *to drain Faenza and Florence of gold and men.)*

According to Nostradamus scholars, the words may signal the arrival of a great Canadian leader, though there's no indication of how long we may have to wait.

# OUT OF THIS WORLD

## What's Cropping Up?

Here's a shocker. If you think crop circles are made by a bunch of drunken British blokes in the English countryside, think again. Not only are these strange geometrical patterns found in almost every country in the world, but Canada is also one of those countries! Since 1925, over 265 reports of unexplained crop circle formations have been documented in Canadian provinces. Most occur in the prairies, but crop circles have been discovered in British Columbia, Ontario, Québec and even the Maritimes. Oral reports go back to at least the 1920s, when farmers recounted circular patterns of swirled, downed plants in all types of crops as well as wild grasses.

Even before the British crop circles made headlines in the late 1980s, Canada had photographs and eyewitness accounts of similar crop circle formations. One such occurred on a rainy September day in 1974, when farmer Edwin Fuhr decided to go out and harvest his rapeseed crop in Langenburg, Saskatchewan.

All was going as usual until he suddenly noticed a steel-coloured object hovering above the ground and spinning in a clockwise direction. He then saw four more similar objects in the air, all spinning. One even seemed to probe something into the ground. This strange sight went on for about 15 minutes before the objects ascended into the sky and took off, leaving behind five "crop circles." The vegetation was not harmed, merely flattened in an overlapping, clockwise pattern.

When Fuhr told his father and brother-in-law, they examined the crop circles together and decided to call the RCMP. The RCMP constable, who knew the Fuhrs, took photographs but could not explain the circles, nor did he think it was just a hoax on Edwin Fuhr's part. Two days later, another circle inexplicably appeared next to the original five, and by mid-September, a seventh had "cropped up." Locals also reported unusually agitated cattle and other circular formations in neighbouring towns. It was undoubtedly a strange harvest that year.

## What Happened to the Beef?
It's not exactly dinner conversation, but Canada has seen its share of a bizarre and mysterious occurrence—cattle mutilations. Yes, reports of deceased, disfigured and generally cut-open bovines are made every once in a while. Just ask Fern Belzil. As a cattle rancher near St. Paul, Alberta, he knows his cows but doesn't know why some end up as bona fide cattle mutilation cases, or "mutes" as he calls them. Belzil has studied the phenomenon for over two decades and agrees that many mutilation reports simply turn out to be the work of a natural predator.

That being said, he's seen enough strange mutilations to be convinced that something else is going on out in the fields. A cow or heifer is found dead in the pasture, all four limbs sticking straight up. Its back might be broken, as if dropped from the air. The animal may also be missing body parts, such as the brain, rectum or reproductive organs, or have its head stripped of flesh, right down to the bone. Other telltale signs include an absence of blood, perhaps with a puncture wound in the jugular vein—whoever, or whatever, does this obviously possesses a certain degree of anatomical knowledge. Mutes do not show signs of a struggle or bite marks but rather have cuts on their bodies that seem to have been made with clean, surgical precision, as if the wounds were sealed or cauterized to prevent any blood spillage. Can a wolf operate a medical laser?

Even weirder, there have been reports of UFOs or unmarked black helicopters in the area of cattle mutilations. Is there a secret government conspiracy, or perhaps a connection between the mutilations and mad cow disease? What's the explanation? Are aliens harvesting bovine DNA? Only the cows know for sure, and they're, well, "mute" about it.

## It's a CUFO…a Canadian UFO!

Canada has one of the highest rates of unidentified flying object (yes, as in UFO) reports per capita in the world. And one in 10 Canadians also admit to having seen a UFO. Of course, the objects these people may have seen could be explained away as aircraft, meteors, space junk—even the planet Venus—but some accounts are much harder to explain away. Native legends often mention "star people," which could be construed as extraterrestrial visitors. In 1663, Jesuit missionaries in New France, now Québec, wrote of watching "…fiery Serpents, intertwined in the form of Caduceus, and flying through mid-air, borne on wings of flame…" The reports continue, such as one from 1796, when a Loyalist merchant recorded "…a strange story is going that a fleet of ships have been seen in the air in some part of the Bay of Fundy…" Fleet of ships in the air?

Fast forward to 1845, and an even stranger case is documented. On a September night that year at Marsh Point Farm, near

Cornwall, Ontario, dozens of people witnessed strange lights and accompanying "explosive" sounds. The light show continued sporadically for about a year before slowly fading away, but the occurrence was never adequately explained. Nor was the first UFO photograph taken on July 10, 1947—it happened near Harmon Field, a U.S. Air Force Base stationed in Newfoundland. Two airplane mechanics took the photo, which showed a silver disc with a long smoke trail. American officials at the time were concerned it might be a Soviet craft, but it wasn't, and no one ever found out what it was exactly.

### The Best Canadian UFO Cases

Canada is not immune from those unexplainable UFO flaps. We've had our fair share of strange lights in the sky. What's more, many accounts were documented and have yet to be resolved. Today, there is even a UFOlogy Research Centre in Winnipeg, Manitoba, ready to take down any new accounts of UFOs. Here's a sampling of what's been going down (or is that up?) in Canadian skies:

*February 15, 1915—Ottawa, Ontario:* Strange aerial objects, as well as unexplained beams of light and even whirring sounds, were seen and heard by eyewitnesses from Brockville to Gananoque throughout the evening of February 14. After being assured that this wasn't an impromptu Valentine's Day fireworks display, Prime Minister Robert Borden was alerted, and the lights on Parliament Hill and most of the city of Ottawa were turned off. Since this was during World War I and there had been raids on Britain, the fear was that some sort of enemy aircraft was about to attack Canada's capital.

*June 29, 1954—Goose Bay, Newfoundland:* The pilot and crew of a BOAC Stratocruiser passenger plane en route from New York to London observed a large pear-shaped craft morph into a "flying arrow." Six smaller unidentified objects moved around it and finally merged into this mothership, which the pilot commented was as large as the transatlantic cruiser, the *Queen Mary*. It then sped away at a high rate of speed. The entire incident lasted about 18 minutes.

*August 23, 1956—Fort Macleod, Alberta:* RCAP Squadron Leader Robert Childrehose was performing a speed record in his Sabre jet over Fort Macleod, Alberta, when he and his flight lieutenant saw a bright oval UFO. They even had time to photograph the object. Five years earlier, a U.S. Navy transport plane reported that it had almost hit a similar, bright, round, orange orb between Iceland and Newfoundland.

*January 25, 2010—Harbour Mille, Newfoundland:* A blurry, missile-like object is spotted by a local resident, and she takes a great photo of it. The RCMP investigates, and the Prime Minister's Office later confirms that it wasn't a missile but had no idea what it was.

## The Curious Case of Stefan Michalak

Something very strange happened to amateur prospector Stefan Michalak on May 20, 1967—and he had the burns on his chest to prove it. When he left the Falcon Lake Motel in Manitoba that morning, the 50-year-old Michalak had no idea how unusual his day was about to be. Wearing welder goggles to protect his eyes from chips, Michalak was inspecting rock formations when he heard the sound of startled geese. He looked up in time to see two red, glowing, cigar-shaped objects floating in the air. They slowly approached, changed to more oval shapes and hovered until one landed on a nearby rock. Partially hidden, Michalak still had an amazing view of the event and stared for about half an hour while the craft changed from a red, then orange and finally to a greyish colour. He even had time to sketch the object, which he estimated to be about 12 metres in diameter. Michalak made note of the sulphury odour, warm air and strange hissing sounds that seemed to be emanating from it.

When a door on the craft suddenly opened, Michalak described what sounded like two people talking. Had he stumbled on some sort of test aircraft? Michalak walked toward the craft and called out in English and a few other languages. The voices stopped, but by this time Michalak was close enough to peer through the doorway and glimpse flashing lights inside. When he stepped back, three panels immediately snapped shut and sealed the opening. Michalak touched the outside of the craft and noted that it felt like smooth, coloured glass but was also hot enough to melt his rubber glove. The craft suddenly began to turn, and hot air shot out from what seemed like a vent right toward Michalak's chest, burning his shirt in the process. The craft climbed into the sky and disappeared, leaving behind a circular pile of dirt and leaves.

Soon after, Michalak developed a painful headache and nausea, but he was able to make his way back to the motel and then went to Winnipeg. Over the next few weeks, doctors in Canada and even the Mayo Clinic in Minnesota were unable to explain his symptoms, which sounded suspiciously like radiation poisoning. Strangest of all are the "burn" marks arranged like a series of dots across his chest. Did they come from the "vent" on the craft and the blast of hot air? Despite being one of the best-documented

cases involving UFOs, neither the RCMP, the Royal Canadian Air Force, nor any of the various departments of health and welfare that examined Stefan Michalak were able to explain exactly what happened that day.

## Canada's Roswell

Unless you've been living under a rock the past few decades, you've likely heard of Roswell, New Mexico, the small American town where an alien craft allegedly crashed in early July 1947. What you may not know is that 20 years later, something else fell from the sky into Shag Harbour in southern Nova Scotia, which, like Roswell, caused quite a commotion at the time. The events were largely forgotten until the late 1990s when researchers took another look at this unusual and unexplained event. One researcher, who actually witnessed the Shag Harbour incident as a 12-year-old boy, later wrote about his experience in a book. What follows is a bizarre story with no clear explanation, just like Roswell.

It began early in the evening of October 4, 1967, when the crew of an Air Canada DC-8 flying over Québec took note of a bright, rectangular object being followed by smaller lights in the sky;

the event was observed for several minutes. A short time later, eyewitnesses in the Maritimes, including a Nova Scotia fishing vessel captain, also reported seeing strange lights in the sky, including a glowing orange ball and a formation of lights in a triangular pattern. The sightings continued until approximately 11:20 PM, when several people said they heard a loud bang, saw a flash of light and knew something had hit the water. Thinking it may have been a crashed aircraft, calls were made to the local RCMP, who were soon on site. An odd, yellowish light was illuminating the water from below, surrounded by a peculiar, brightly coloured foam. By the time the RCMP reached the object, however, it had sunk well below the surface. The next day, divers combed the area for debris. Nothing was found, officially at least, but rumours circulated that a mysterious metallic material had indeed been recovered. To this day, the Department of National Defence says the case remains unresolved. Whether it was a secret military aircraft, a crashed satellite or simply a meteorite, we may never know. Thanks to reports from various authorities—the RCMP, the City of Halifax and even the Canadian Air Force—Shag Harbour remains a true, well-documented, unidentified flying object event.

 Flashback to 1977—NASA launches *Voyager I* and *Voyager II*, two interstellar probes embarking on their journey throughout the universe. On board each probe is a gold disc, the Voyager Interstellar Record, which contains the history of Earth in images and sound. The audio portion includes the voices of two Canadians, as well as a J.S. Bach composition performed by Canadian pianist Glenn Gould. Of the 115 analogue images, however, only one is of Canada. No, it wasn't the Horseshoe Falls at Niagara, the Rocky Mountains in Banff or any other majestic Canadian scene—it was an aerial view of the Toronto airport.

# CONCLUSION

Well, there you have it—a collection of some of the most bizarre people, places and events in this great country of ours. The lists on these preceding pages are by no means complete, and I'm sure there's a lot more bizarre Canadiana out there that could fill several volumes, and undoubtedly there are many, many more books to come. If there's one thing I know for certain, it's that bizarre stuff is always happening, and weird, curious, unusual and generally crazy stuff happens *all the time*, especially here in Canada. So keep an eye out and embrace the eccentricities around us—we're Canadian after all, and yep, we're blessed to be bizarre.

# NOTES ON SOURCES

Wow, researching for this book was a formidable but thoroughly enjoyable mission. There's so much information online that I could easily spend the rest of my life looking up bizarre Canadian facts. Thank heavens so many journal and newspaper articles can still be accessed through public library databases, and Wikipedia and Google—I love you both even if I have to delve elsewhere to double check your words! Other sites I found particularly helpful were www.collectionscanada.ca, www.mysteriesofcanada.com, www.canadacool.com and www.archives.cbc.ca. The following books were also used:

Colombo, John Robert. *Mysterious Canada: Strange Sights, Extraordinary Events, and Peculiar Places*. Toronto: Doubleday, 1988.

Dittman, Geoff and Chris Rutkowski. *The Canadian UFO Report: The Best Cases Revealed*. Toronto: Dundurn Press, 2006.

Grady, Wayne. *Chasing the Chinook: On the Trail of Canadian Words and Culture*. Toronto: Viking, 1998.

Hancock, Pat. *Crazy Canadian Trivia*. Toronto: Scholastic Canada, 2000.

—. *Crazy Canadian Trivia 2*. Toronto: Scholastic Canada, 2005.

—. *Crazy Canadian Trivia 3*. Toronto: Scholastic Canada, 2008.

—. *Crazy Canadian Trivia 4*. Toronto, Scholastic Canada, 2009.

Hoshowsky, Robert. *The Last to Die*. Toronto: Dundurn Press, 2007.

Kearney, Mark and Randy Ray. *The Great Canadian Trivia Book 2*. Toronto: Hounslow Press, 1998.

—. *The Big Book of Canadian Trivia*. Toronto: Dundurn Press, 2009.

Liss, Nancy and Ted Liss. *Curious Canadians*. Markham, ON: Fitzhenry & Whiteside, 2002.

Richmond, Randy and Tom Villemarie. *Colossal Canadian Failures: A Short History of Things That Seemed Like a Good Idea at the Time*. Toronto: Dundurn Press, 2002.

—. *Colossal Canadian Failures 2: A Short History of Things That Seemed Like a Good Idea at the Time*. Toronto: Dundurn Press, 2006.

Stafford, David. *Camp X: SOE and the American Connection*. New York: Viking Books, 1986.

Wallechinsky, David, et al. *The Book of Lists: The Original Compendium of Curious Information*. Toronto: Alfred Knopf, 2005.

# ABOUT THE ILLUSTRATORS

### Roger Garcia

Roger Garcia is a self-taught artist with some formal training who specializes in cartooning and illustration. He is an immigrant from El Salvador, and during the last few years, his work has been primarily cartoons and editorial illustrations in pen and ink. Recently, he has started painting once more, focusing on simplifying the human form, using a bright minimal palette and as few elements as possible. His work can be seen in newspapers, magazines and promo material and on www.rogergarcia.ca.

### Peter Tyler

Peter is a graduate of the Vancouver Film School's Visual Art and Design and Classical animation programs. Though his ultimate passion is in filmmaking, he is also intent on developing his draftsmanship and storytelling, with the aim of using those skills in future filmic misadventures.

### Patrick Hénaff

A native of France, Patrick Hénaff is mostly self-taught and is a versatile artist who has explored a variety of mediums under many different influences. He now uses primarily pen and ink to draw and then processes the images on computer. He is particularly interested in the narrative power of pictures and tries to use them as a way to tell stories, whether he is working on comic pages, posters, illustrations, cartoons or concept art.